# THE LOVE DARE

Presented to

_____

By

_____

_____

_____

Date

_____

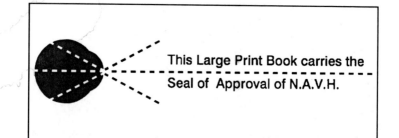

This Large Print Book carries the
Seal of Approval of N.A.V.H.

# THE LOVE DARE

## STEPHEN AND ALEX KENDRICK
### *with Lawrence Kimbrough*

**CHRISTIAN LARGE PRINT**
*A part of Gale, Cengage Learning*

GALE
CENGAGE Learning

Detroit • New York • San Francisco • New Haven, Conn • Waterville, Maine • London

**GALE**
CENGAGE Learning

Copyright © 2008 by Stephen Kendrick & Alex Kendrick.
Unless otherwise noted, all Scripture quotations are taken from the
*New American Standard Bible®*, Copyright © 1960, 1962, 1963, 1968,
1971, 1972, 1973, 1975, 1977, 1995 by The Lockman Foundation. Used
by permission.
Other versions used include: *Holman Christian Standard Bible®*
Copyright © 1999, 2000, 2002, 2003 by Holman Bible Publishers. Used
by permission. *New International Version®* Copyright © 1973, 1978,
1984 International Bible Society. Used by permission of Zondervan. All
rights reserved. *New King James Version,* Copyright © 1982 by Thomas
Nelson, Inc. Used by permission. All rights reserved.
Christian Large Print, a part of Gale, Cengage Learning.

**ALL RIGHTS RESERVED**
Christian Large Print Originals.
The text of this Large Print edition is unabridged.
Other aspects of the book may vary from the original edition.
Set in 16 pt. Plantin.
Printed on permanent paper.

**LIBRARY OF CONGRESS CATALOGING-IN-PUBLICATION DATA**

Kendrick, Stephen, 1973–
  The love dare / by Stephen & Alex Kendrick ; with Lawrence
Kimbrough.
    p. cm.
  ISBN-13: 978-1-59415-297-9 (pbk. : alk. paper)
  ISBN-10: 1-59415-297-7 (pbk. : alk. paper)
  1. Spouses—Prayers and devotions. 2. Marriage—Religious
aspects—Christianity—Textbooks. 3. Large type books. I.
Kendrick, Alex, 1970– II. Kimbrough, Lawrence, 1963– III. Title.
BV4596.M3K45 2009
242'.644—dc22
                                                    2009018414

Published in 2009 by arrangement with Riggins International Rights
Services, Inc.

Printed in the United States of America
2  3  4  5  6     16 15 14 13 12
FD172

Receive this as a warning. This forty day journey cannot be taken lightly.

It is a challenging and often difficult process, but an incredibly fulfilling one. To take this dare requires a resolute mind and a steadfast determination.

It is not meant to be sampled or briefly tested, and those who quit early will forfeit the greatest benefits. If you will commit to a day at a time for forty days, the results could change your life and your marriage.

Consider it a dare, from others who have done it before you.

The Scriptures say that God designed and created marriage as a good thing. It is a beautiful, priceless gift. He uses marriage to help us eliminate loneliness, multiply our effectiveness, establish families, raise children, enjoy life, and bless us with relational intimacy. But beyond this, marriage also shows us our need to grow and deal with our own issues and self-centeredness through the help of a lifelong partner. If we are teachable, we will learn to do the one thing that is most important in marriage — to love. This powerful union provides the path for you to learn how to love another imperfect person unconditionally. It is wonderful. It is difficult. It is life changing.

This book is about love. It's about learning and daring to live a life filled with loving relationships. And this journey begins with the person who is closest to you: your spouse. May God bless you as you begin this adventure.

But be sure of this: it will take courage. If you accept this dare, you must take the view that instead of *following* your heart, you are choosing to *lead it.* The world says to follow your heart, but if you are not leading it, then someone or something else is. The Bible says that "the heart is more deceitful than all else" (Jeremiah 17:9), and it will always pursue that which feels right at the moment.

We dare you to think differently — choosing instead to *lead your heart* toward that which is best in the long run. This is a key to lasting, fulfilling relationships.

The Love Dare journey is not a process of trying to change your spouse to be the person you want them to be. You've no doubt already discovered that efforts to change your husband or wife have ended in failure and frustration. Rather, this is a journey of exploring and demonstrating genuine love, even when your desire is dry and your motives are low. The truth is, love is a decision and not just a feeling. It is selfless, sacrificial, and transformational. And when love is truly demonstrated as it was intended, your relationship is more likely to change for the better.

Each day of this journey will contain three very important elements:

**First,** a unique aspect of love will be discussed. Read each of these carefully and be open to a new understanding of what it means to genuinely love someone.

**Second,** you will be given a specific dare to do for your spouse. Some will be easy and some very challenging. But take each dare seriously, and be creative and courageous enough to attempt it. Don't be discouraged if outside situations prevent you from accomplishing a specific dare. Just pick back up as soon as you can and proceed with the journey.

**Last,** you will be given journal space to log what you are learning and doing and how your spouse is responding. It is important that you take advantage of this space to capture what is happening to both you and your mate along the way. These notes will record your progress and should become priceless to you in the future.

Remember, you have the responsibility to protect and guide your heart. Don't give up and don't get discouraged. Resolve to lead your heart and to make it through to the end. Learning to truly love is one of the most important things you will ever do.

NOW THESE THREE REMAIN:
FAITH, HOPE, AND LOVE.
BUT THE GREATEST OF THESE IS LOVE
*1 Corinthians 13:13*

If I speak with the tongues of men and of angels, but do not have love, I have become a noisy gong or a clanging cymbal.

If I have the gift of prophecy, and know all mysteries and all knowledge; and if I have all faith, so as to remove mountains, but do not have love, I am nothing.

And if I give all my possessions to feed the poor, and if I surrender my body to be burned, but do not have love, it profits me nothing.

1 CORINTHIANS 13:1–3

# DAY 1
## LOVE IS PATIENT

Be completely humble and gentle; be
patient, bearing with one another in love.
— Ephesians 4:2 NIV

Love works. It is life's most powerful moti-
vator and has far greater depth and meaning than most people realize. It always does
what is best for others and can empower us
to face the greatest of problems. We are born
with a lifelong thirst for love. Our hearts
desperately need it like our lungs need
oxygen. Love changes our motivation for
living. Relationships become meaningful
with it. No marriage is successful without
it.

Love is built on two pillars that best define
what it is. Those pillars are *patience* and
*kindness.* All other characteristics of love
are extensions of these two attributes. And
that's where your dare will begin. With *patience.*

Love will inspire you to become a patient person. When you choose to be patient, you respond in a positive way to a negative situation. You are slow to anger. You choose to have a long fuse instead of a quick temper. Rather than being restless and demanding, love helps you settle down and begin extending mercy to those around you. Patience brings an internal calm during an external storm.

No one likes to be around an impatient person. It causes you to overreact in angry, foolish, and regrettable ways. The irony of anger toward a wrongful action is that it spawns new wrongs of its own. *Anger* almost never makes things better. In fact, it usually generates additional problems. But *patience* stops problems in their tracks. More than biting your lip, more than clapping a hand over your mouth, patience is a deep breath. It clears the air. It stops foolishness from whipping its scorpion tail all over the room. It is a choice to control your emotions rather than allowing your emotions to control you, and shows discretion instead of returning evil for evil.

If your spouse offends you, do you quickly retaliate, or do you stay under control? Do you find that anger is your emotional default when treated unfairly? If so, you are spreading poison rather than medicine.

Anger is usually caused when the strong desire for something is mixed with disappointment or grief. You don't get what you want and you start heating up inside. It is often an emotional reaction that flows out of our own selfishness, foolishness, or evil motives.

Patience, however, makes us wise. It doesn't rush to judgment but listens to what the other person is saying. Patience stands in the doorway where anger is clawing to burst in, but waits to see the whole picture before passing judgment. The Bible says, "He who is slow to anger has great understanding, but he who is quick-tempered exalts folly" (Proverbs 14:29).

As sure as a lack of patience will turn your home into a war zone, the practice of patience will foster peace and quiet. "A hot-tempered man stirs up strife, but the slow to anger calms a dispute" (Proverbs 15:18). Statements like these from the Bible book of Proverbs are clear principles with timeless relevance. Patience is where love meets wisdom. And every marriage needs that combination to stay healthy.

Patience helps you give your spouse permission to be human. It understands that everyone fails. When a mistake is made, it chooses to give them more time than they deserve to correct it. It gives you the ability to hold on during the tough times in your relationship rather than bailing out under the pressure.

But can your spouse count on having a patient wife or husband to deal with? Can she know that locking her keys in the car will be met by your understanding rather than a demeaning lecture that makes her feel like a child? Can he know that cheering during the last seconds of a football game won't invite a loud-mouthed laundry list of ways he should be spending his time? It turns out that few people are as hard to live with as an impatient person.

What would the tone and volume of your home be like if you tried this biblical approach: "See that no one repays another with evil for evil, but always seek after that which is good for one another" (1 Thessalonians 5:15).

Few of us do patience very well, and none of us do it naturally. But wise men and women will pursue it as an essential ingredient to their marriage relationships. That's a good starting point to demonstrate true love.

This Love Dare journey is a process, and the first thing you must resolve to possess is patience. Think of it as a marathon, not a sprint. But it's a race worth running.

## Today's Dare

THE FIRST PART OF THIS DARE IS FAIRLY SIMPLE. ALTHOUGH LOVE IS COMMUNICATED IN A NUMBER OF WAYS, OUR WORDS OFTEN REFLECT THE CONDITION OF OUR HEART. FOR THE NEXT DAY, RESOLVE TO DEMONSTRATE PATIENCE AND TO SAY NOTHING NEGATIVE TO YOUR SPOUSE AT ALL. IF THE TEMPTATION ARISES, CHOOSE NOT TO SAY ANYTHING. IT'S BETTER TO HOLD YOUR TONGUE THAN TO SAY SOMETHING YOU'LL REGRET.

__ Check here when you've completed today's dare.

Did anything happen today to cause anger toward your mate? Were you tempted to think disapproving thoughts and to let them come out in words?

_____

_____

_____

_____

_____

_____

_____

_____

_____

_____

_____

_____

_____

_____

_____

_____

*Everyone must be quick to hear, slow to speak and slow to anger. (James 1:19)*

# DAY 2
## LOVE IS KIND

Be kind to one another, tender-hearted, forgiving each other, just as God in Christ also has forgiven you. — Ephesians 4:32

Kindness is love in action. If patience is how love *reacts* in order to minimize a negative circumstance, kindness is how love *acts* to maximize a positive circumstance. Patience avoids a problem; kindness creates a blessing. One is preventive, the other proactive. These two sides of love are the cornerstones on which many of the other attributes we will discuss are built.

Love makes you kind. And kindness makes you likeable. When you're kind, people want to be around you. They see you as being good *to* them and good *for* them.

The Bible keys in on the importance of kindness: "Do not let kindness and truth leave you; bind them around your neck, write them on the tablet of your heart. So you will find favor and good repute in the sight of God and man" (Proverbs 3:3–4). Kind people simply find favor wherever they go. Even at home. But "kindness" can feel a little generic when you try defining it, much less living it. So let's break kindness down into four basic core ingredients:

*Gentleness.* When you're operating from kindness, you're careful how you treat your spouse, never being unnecessarily harsh. You're sensitive. Tender. Even if you need to say hard things, you'll bend over backwards to make your rebuke or challenge as easy to hear as possible. You speak the truth in love.

*Helpfulness.* Being kind means you meet the needs of the moment. If it's housework, you get busy. A listening ear? You give it. Kindness graces a wife with the ability to serve her husband without worrying about her rights. Kindness makes a husband curious to discover what his wife needs, then motivates him to be the one who steps up and ensures those needs are met — even if his are put on hold.

*Willingness.* Kindness inspires you to be agreeable. Instead of being obstinate, reluc-

tant, or stubborn, you cooperate
flexible. Rather than complaining
ing excuses, you look for reasons
mise and accommodate. A kin
ends thousands of potential arguments by
his willingness to listen first rather than
demand his way.

*Initiative.* Kindness thinks ahead, then takes
the first step. It doesn't sit around waiting
to be prompted or coerced before getting
off the couch. The kind husband or wife
will be the one who greets first, smiles first,
serves first, and forgives first. They don't
require the other to get his or her act
together before showing love. When acting
from kindness, you see the need, then make
your move. First.

Jesus creatively described the kindness of
love in His parable of the Good Samaritan,
found in the Bible — Luke, chapter 10. A
Jewish man attacked by robbers is left for
dead on a remote road. Two religious leaders, respected among their people, walk by
without choosing to stop. Too busy. Too
important. Too fond of clean hands. But a
common man of another race — the hated
Samaritans, whose dislike for the Jews was
both bitter and mutual — sees this stranger

eed and is moved with compassion. rossing all cultural boundaries and risking ridicule, he stops to help the man. Bandaging his wounds and putting him on his own donkey, he carries him to safety and pays all his medical expenses out of his own pocket.

Where years of racism had caused strife and division, one act of kindness brought two enemies together. Gently. Helpfully. Willingly. Taking the initiative, this man demonstrated true kindness in every way.

Wasn't kindness one of the key things that drew you and your spouse together in the first place? When you married, weren't you expecting to enjoy his or her kindness for the rest of your life? Didn't your mate feel the same way about you? Even though the years can take the edge off that desire, your enjoyment in marriage is still linked to the daily level of kindness expressed.

The Bible describes a woman whose husband and children bless and praise her. Among her noble attributes are these: "She opens her mouth in wisdom, and the teaching of kindness is on her tongue" (Proverbs 31:26). How about you? How would your husband or wife describe you on the kindness meter? How harsh are you? How gentle and helpful? Do you wait to be asked, or do you take the initiative to help? Don't wait for your spouse to be kind first.

It is difficult to demonstrate love when you feel little to no motivation. But love in its truest sense is not based on feelings. Rather, love determines to show thoughtful actions even when there seems to be no reward. You will never learn to love until you learn to demonstrate kindness.

## TODAY'S DARE

IN ADDITION TO SAYING NOTHING NEGA-
TIVE TO YOUR SPOUSE AGAIN TODAY, DO
AT LEAST ONE UNEXPECTED GESTURE AS
AN ACT OF KINDNESS.

__ Check here when you've completed
today's dare.

What discoveries about love did you make
today? What specifically did you do in this
dare? How did you show kindness?

_____

_____

_____

_____

_____

_____

_____

_____

_____

_____

_____

_____

_____

_____

_____

_____

_____

_____

_____

_____

*What is desirable in a man is his*
*kindness. (Proverbs 19:22)*

# DAY 3
## LOVE IS NOT SELFISH

Be devoted to one another in brotherly love; give preference to one another in honor. — Romans 12:10

We live in a world that is enamored with "self." The culture around us teaches us to focus on our appearance, feelings, and personal desires as the top priority. The goal, it seems, is to chase the highest level of happiness possible. The danger from this kind of thinking, however, becomes painfully apparent once inside a marriage relationship.

If there were ever a word that basically means the opposite of love, it is *selfishness*. Unfortunately it is something that is ingrained into every person from birth. You can see it in the way young children act, and often in the way adults mistreat one another. Almost every sinful action ever committed can be traced back to a selfish motive. It is a trait we hate in other people but justify in ourselves. Yet you cannot point out the many ways your spouse is selfish without admitting that you can be selfish too. That would be hypocritical.

Why do we have such low standards for ourselves but high expectations for our mate? The answer is a painful pill to swallow. *We are all selfish.*

When a husband puts his interests, desires, and priorities in front of his wife, that's a sign of selfishness. When a wife constantly complains about the time and energy she spends meeting the needs of her husband, that's a sign of selfishness. But love "does not seek its own" (1 Corinthians 13:5). Loving couples — the ones who are enjoying the full purpose of marriage — are bent on taking good care of the other flawed human they get to share life with. That's because true love looks for ways to say "yes."

One ironic aspect of selfishness is that even generous actions can be selfish if the motive is to gain bragging rights or receive a reward. If you do even a good thing to deceitfully manipulate your husband or wife, you are still being selfish. The bottom line is that you either make decisions out of love for others or love for yourself.

Love is never satisfied except in the welfare

of others. You can't be acting out of real love and selfishness at the same time. Choosing to love your mate will cause you to say "no" to what you want so you can say "yes" to what they need. That's putting the happiness of your partner above your own. It doesn't mean you can never experience happiness, but you don't negate the happiness of your spouse so you can enjoy it yourself.

Love also leads to inner joy. When you prioritize the well-being of your mate, there is a resulting fulfillment that cannot be duplicated by selfish actions. This is a benefit that God created and reserves for those who genuinely demonstrate love. The truth is, when you relinquish your rights for the sake of your mate, you get a chance to lose yourself to the greater purpose of marriage.

Nobody knows you as well as your spouse. And that means no one will be quicker to recognize a change when you deliberately start sacrificing your wants and wishes to make sure his or her needs are met.

If you find it hard to sacrifice your own desires to benefit your spouse, then you may have a deeper problem with selfishness than you want to admit.

Ask yourself these questions:

- Do I truly want what's best for my husband or wife?
- Do I want them to feel loved by me?
- Do they believe I have their best interests in mind?
- Do they see me as looking out for myself first?

Whether you like it or not, you have a reputation in the eyes of those around you, especially in the eyes of your spouse. But is it a loving reputation? Remember, your marriage partner also has the challenge of loving a selfish person. So determine to be the first to demonstrate real love to them, with your eyes wide open. And when all is said and done, you'll both be more fulfilled.

"Do nothing from selfishness or empty conceit, but with humility of mind regard one another as more important than yourselves" (Philippians 2:3).

## TODAY'S DARE

WHATEVER YOU PUT YOUR TIME, ENERGY, AND MONEY INTO WILL BECOME MORE IMPORTANT TO YOU. IT'S HARD TO CARE FOR SOMETHING YOU ARE NOT INVESTING IN. ALONG WITH RESTRAINING FROM NEGATIVE COMMENTS, BUY YOUR SPOUSE SOMETHING THAT SAYS, "I WAS THINKING OF YOU TODAY."

\_\_ Check here when you've completed today's dare.

What did you choose to give your spouse? What happened when you gave it?

_____

_____

_____

_____

_____

_____

_____

_Where jealousy and selfish ambition exist,
there is disorder. (James 3:16)_

# Day 4
## Love is Thoughtful

How precious also are Your thoughts to me. . . . How vast is the sum of them! If I should count them, they would outnumber the sand. — Psalm 139:17–18

Love thinks. It's not a mindless feeling that rides on waves of emotion and falls asleep mentally. It keeps busy in thought, knowing that loving thoughts precede loving actions.

When you first fell in love, being thoughtful came quite naturally. You spent hours dreaming of what your loved one looked like, wondering what he or she was doing, rehearsing impressive things to say, then enjoying sweet memories of the time you spent together. You honestly confessed, "I can't stop thinking about you."

But for most couples, things begin to change after marriage. The wife finally has her man; the husband has his trophy. The hunt is over and the pursuing done. Sparks

36

of romance slowly burn into grey embers, and the motivation for thoughtfulness cools. You drift into focusing on your job, your friends, your problems, your personal desires, yourself. After a while, you unintentionally begin to ignore the needs of your mate.

But the fact that marriage has added another person to your universe does not change. Therefore, if your thinking doesn't mature enough to constantly include this person, you catch yourself being surprised rather than being thoughtful.

"Today's our anniversary?"

"Why didn't you include me in that decision?"

"Don't you ever think about anyone but yourself?"

If you don't learn to be thoughtful, you end up regretting missed opportunities to demonstrate love. Thoughtlessness is a silent enemy to a loving relationship.

Let's be honest. Men struggle with thoughtfulness more than women. A man can focus like a laser on one thing and forget the rest of the world. Whereas this can benefit him in that one arena, it can make him overlook other things that need his attention.

A woman, on the other hand, is more

multi-conscious, able to maintain an amazing awareness of many factors at once. She can talk on the phone, cook, know where the kids are in the house, and wonder why her husband isn't helping . . . all simultaneously. Adding to this, a woman also thinks relationally. When she works on something, she is cognizant of all the people who are somehow connected to it.

Both of these tendencies are examples of how God designed women to complete their men. As God said at creation, "It is not good for the man to be alone; I will make him a helper suitable for him" (Genesis 2:18). But these differences also create opportunities for misunderstanding.

Men, for example, tend to think in headlines and say exactly what they mean. Not much is needed to understand the message. His words are more literal and shouldn't be over-analyzed. But women think and speak between the lines. They tend to hint. A man often has to listen for what is implied if he wants to get the full meaning.

If a couple doesn't understand this about one another, the fallout can result in endless disagreements. He's frustrated wondering why she speaks in riddles and doesn't just come out and say things. She's frustrated wondering why he's so inconsiderate and doesn't add two and two together and just figure it out.

A woman deeply longs for her husband to be thoughtful. It is a key to helping her feel loved. When she speaks, a wise man will listen like a detective to discover the unspoken needs and desires her words imply. If, however, she always has to put the pieces together for him, it steals the opportunity for him to demonstrate that he loves her.

This also explains why women will get upset with their husbands without telling them why. In her mind she's thinking, "I shouldn't have to spell it out for him. He should be able to look at the situation and see what's going on here." At the same time, he's grieved because he can't read her mind and wonders why he's being punished for a crime he didn't know he committed.

Love requires thoughtfulness — on both sides — the kind that builds bridges through the constructive combination of patience, kindness, and selflessness. Love teaches you how to meet in the middle, to respect and appreciate how your spouse uniquely thinks.

A husband should listen to his wife and learn to be considerate of her unspoken messages. A wife should learn to communicate truthfully and not say one thing while meaning another.

But too often you become angry and frustrated instead, following the destructive pattern of "ready, shoot, aim." You speak harshly now and determine later if you should have said it. But the thoughtful nature of love teaches you to engage your mind before engaging your lips. Love thinks before speaking. It filters words through a grid of truth and kindness.

When was the last time you spent a few minutes thinking about how you could better understand and demonstrate love to your spouse? What immediate need can you meet? What's the next event (anniversary, birthday, holiday) you could be preparing for? Great marriages come from great thinking.

## TODAY'S DARE

CONTACT YOUR SPOUSE SOMETIME DURING THE BUSINESS OF THE DAY. HAVE NO AGENDA OTHER THAN ASKING HOW HE OR SHE IS DOING AND IF THERE IS ANYTHING YOU COULD DO FOR THEM.

___ Check here when you've completed today's dare.

What did you learn about yourself or your spouse by doing this today? How could this become a more natural, routine, and genuinely helpful part of your lifestyle?

_____

_____

_____

_____

_____

_____

_____

_____

_____

_____

_____

_____

_____

_____

_____

_____

_____

_____

*I thank my God in all my remembrance of you. (Philippians 1:3)*

43

# Day 5
## Love is not rude

He who blesses his friend with a loud
voice early in the morning, it will be
reckoned a curse to him.
— Proverbs 27:14

Nothing irritates others as quickly as being
rude. Rudeness is unnecessarily saying or
doing things that are unpleasant for another
person to be around. To be rude is to act
unbecoming, embarrassing, or irritating. In
marriage, this could be a foul mouth, poor
table manners, or a habit of making sarcastic
quips. However you look at it, no one enjoys
being around a rude person. Rude behavior
may seem insignificant to the person doing
it, but it's unpleasant to those on the receiving end.

As always, love has something to say about
this. When a man is driven by love, he
intentionally behaves in a way that's more
pleasant for his wife to be around. If she

desires to love him, she purposefully avoids things that frustrate him or cause him discomfort.

The bottom line is that genuine love minds its manners.

Embracing this one concept could add some fresh air to your marriage. Good manners express to your wife or husband, "I value you enough to exercise some self-control around you. I want to be a person who's a pleasure to be with." When you allow love to change your behavior — even in the smallest of ways — you restore an atmosphere of honor to your relationship. People who practice good etiquette tend to raise the respect level of the environment around them.

For the most part, the etiquette you use at home is much different than the kind you employ with friends, or even with total strangers. You may be barking or pouting around the house, but if the front door chimes, you open it all smiling and kind. Yet if you dare to love, you'll also want to give your best to your own. If you don't let love motivate you to make needed changes in your behavior, the quality of your marriage relationship will suffer for it.

Women tend to be much better at certain types of manners than men, though they can be rude in other ways. King Solomon said, "Better to live on a corner of the roof than share a house with a quarrelsome wife" (Proverbs 25:24 NIV). But men especially need to learn this important lesson. The Bible says, "It is well with the man who is gracious" (Psalm 112:5). A man of discretion will find out what is appropriate, then adjust his behavior accordingly.

There are two main reasons why people are rude: *ignorance* and *selfishness.* Neither, of course, is a good thing. A child is born ignorant of etiquette, needing lots of help and training. Adults, however, display their ignorance at another level. You know the rules, but you can be blind to how you break them or be too self-centered to care. In fact, you may not realize how unpleasant you can be to live with.

Test yourself with these questions:

- How does your spouse feel about the way you speak and act around them?
- How does your behavior affect your mate's sense of worth and self-esteem?
- Would your husband or wife say you're a blessing, or that you're condescending and embarrassing?

If you're thinking that your spouse — not you — is the one who needs work in this area, you're likely suffering from a bad case of ignorance, with a secondary condition of selfishness. Remember, love is not rude but lifts you to a higher standard.

Do you wish your spouse would quit doing the things that bother you? Then it's time to stop doing the things that bother them. Will you be thoughtful and loving enough to discover and avoid the behavior that causes life to be unpleasant for your mate? Will you dare to be delightful?

Here are three guiding principles when it comes to practicing etiquette in your marriage:

1. *Guard the Golden Rule.* Treat your mate the same way you want to be treated (see Luke 6:31).
2. *No double standards.* Be as considerate to your spouse as you are to strangers and coworkers.
3. *Honor requests.* Consider what your husband or wife already asked you to do or not do. If in doubt, then ask.

## TODAY'S DARE

ASK YOUR SPOUSE TO TELL YOU THREE THINGS THAT CAUSE HIM OR HER TO BE UNCOMFORTABLE OR IRRITATED WITH YOU. YOU MUST DO SO WITHOUT ATTACKING THEM OR JUSTIFYING YOUR BEHAVIOR. THIS IS FROM THEIR PERSPECTIVE ONLY.

__ Check here when you've completed today's dare.

What things did your spouse point out about you that need your attention? How did you handle hearing it? What do you plan to do to improve these areas?

_____

_____

_____

_____

_____

_____

The words from the mouth of a wise man
are gracious. (Ecclesiastes 10:12)

# Day 6
## Love is not
### IRRITABLE

He who is slow to anger is better than the mighty, and he who rules his spirit, than he who captures a city. — Proverbs 16:32

Love is hard to offend and quick to forgive. How easily do you get irritated and offended? Some people have the motto, "Never pass up an opportunity to get upset with your spouse." When something goes wrong, they quickly take full advantage of it by expressing how hurt or frustrated they are. But this is the opposite reaction of love.

To be *irritable* means "to be near the point of a knife." Not far from being poked. People who are irritable are locked, loaded, and ready to overreact.

When under pressure, love doesn't turn sour. Minor problems don't yield major reactions. The truth is, love does not get angry or hurt unless there is a legitimate and just reason in the sight of God. A loving husband will remain calm and patient, showing mercy and restraining his temper. Rage and violence are out of the question. A loving wife is not overly sensitive or cranky but exercises emotional self-control. She chooses to be a flower among the thorns and respond pleasantly during prickly situations.

If you are walking under the influence of love, you will be a joy, not a jerk. Ask yourself, "Am I a calming breeze, or a storm waiting to happen?"

Why do people become irritable? There are at least two key reasons that contribute to it:

*Stress.* Stress weighs you down, drains your energy, weakens your health, and invites you to be cranky. It can be brought on by *relational* causes: arguing, division, and bitterness. There are *excessive* causes: overworking, overplaying, and overspending. And there are *deficiencies:* not getting enough rest, nutrition, or exercise. Oftentimes we inflict these daggers on ourselves, and this sets us up to be irritable.

Life is a marathon, not a sprint. This means you must balance, prioritize, and pace yourself. Too often we throw caution to the wind and run full steam ahead, doing what feels right at the moment. Soon we are gasping for air, wound up in knots, and ready to snap. The increasing pressure can wear away at our patience and our relationship.

The Bible can help you avoid unhealthy stress. It teaches you to let love guide your relationships so you aren't caught up in unnecessary arguments (Colossians 3:12–14). To pray through your anxieties instead of tackling them on your own (Philippians 4:6–7). To delegate when you are overworked (Exodus 18:17–23). To avoid overindulgence (Proverbs 25:16).

It also exhorts you to take a "Sabbath" vacation day every week for worship and rest. This strategically allows you time to recharge, refocus, and add breathing room or margin to your weekly schedule. Establishing these kinds of extra spaces will place cushions between you and the pressures around you, reducing the stress that keeps you on edge around your mate. But there is a deeper reason why you can become irritable —

*Selfishness.* When you're irritable, the heart of the problem is primarily a problem of the heart. Jesus said, "Out of the abundance of the heart the mouth speaks" (Matthew 12:34 NKJV). Some people are like lemons: when life squeezes them, they pour out a sour response. Some are more like peaches: when the pressure is on, the result is still sweet.

Being easily angered is an indicator that a hidden area of selfishness or insecurity is present where love is supposed to rule. But selfishness also wears many other masks:

*Lust,* for example, is the result of being ungrateful for what you have and choosing to covet or burn with passion for something that is forbidden. When your heart is lustful, it will become easily frustrated and angered (James 4:1–3). *Bitterness* takes root when you respond in a judgmental way and refuse to work through your anger. A bitter person's unresolved anger leaks out when he is provoked (Ephesians 4:31). *Greed* for more money and possessions will frustrate you with unfulfilled desires (1 Timothy 6:9–10). These strong cravings coupled with dissatisfaction lead you to lash out at anyone who stands in your way. *Pride* leads you to act harshly in order to protect your ego and reputation.

These motivations can never be satisfied. But when love enters your heart, it calms you down and inspires you to quit focusing on yourself. It loosens your grasp and helps you let go of unnecessary things.

Love will lead you to forgive instead of

holding a grudge. To be grateful instead of greedy. To be content rather than rushing into more debt. Love encourages you to be happy when someone else succeeds rather than lying awake at night in envy. Love says "share the inheritance" rather than "fight with your relatives." It reminds you to prioritize your family rather than sacrifice them for a promotion at work. In each decision, love ultimately lowers your stress and helps you release the venom that can build up inside. It then sets up your heart to respond to your spouse with patience and encouragement rather than anger and exasperation.

## TODAY'S DARE

CHOOSE TODAY TO REACT TO TOUGH CIRCUMSTANCES IN YOUR MARRIAGE IN LOVING WAYS INSTEAD OF WITH IRRITATION. BEGIN BY MAKING A LIST BELOW OF AREAS WHERE YOU NEED TO ADD MARGIN TO YOUR SCHEDULE. THEN LIST ANY WRONG MOTIVATIONS THAT YOU NEED TO RELEASE FROM YOUR LIFE.

___ Check here when you've completed today's dare.

Where do you need to add margin to your life? When have you recently overreacted? What was your real motivation behind it? What decisions have you made today?

_____

_____

_____

_____

_____

_____

_____

_____

_____

_____

_____

_____

_____

_____

_____

_____

_____

_____

_____

*I always do my best to have a clear
conscience toward God and men.
(Acts 24:16)*

# DAY 7

## LOVE BELIEVES THE

### BEST

---

[Love] believes all things, hopes all
things. — 1 Corinthians 13:7

In the deep and private corridors of your
heart, there is a room. It's called the Appreciation Room. It's where your thoughts
go when you encounter positive and encouraging things about your spouse. And every
so often, you enjoy visiting this special
place.

On the walls are written kind words and
phrases describing the good attributes of
your mate. These may include characteristics like "honest" and "intelligent," or
phrases like "diligent worker," "wonderful
cook," or "beautiful eyes." They are things
you've discovered about your husband or
wife that have embedded themselves in your
memory. When you think about these things,
your appreciation for your spouse begins to
increase. In fact, the more time you spend

...ing on these positive attributes, the ...e grateful you are for your mate.

Most things in the Appreciation Room were likely written in the initial stages of your relationship. You could summarize them as things you liked and respected about your loved one. They were true, honorable, and good. And you spent a great deal of time dwelling on them in this room . . . before you were married. But you may have found that you don't visit this special room as often as you once did. That's because there is another competing room nearby.

Down another darker corridor of your heart lies the Depreciation Room, and unfortunately you visit there as well.

On its walls are written the things that bother and irritate you about your spouse. These things were placed there out of frustration, hurt feelings, and the disappointment of unmet expectations.

This room is lined with the weaknesses and failures of your husband or wife. Their bad habits, hurtful words, and poor decisions are written in large letters that cover the walls from one end to the other. If you stay in this room long enough, you get depressed and start expressing things like, "My wife is so selfish," or "My husband can be such a jerk." Or maybe, "I think I married the wrong person."

Some people write very hateful things in this room, where tell-off statements are rehearsed for the next argument. Emotional injuries fester here, adding more scathing remarks to the walls. It's where ammunition is kept for the next big fight and bitterness is allowed to spread like a disease. People fall out of love here.

But know this. Spending time in the Depreciation Room kills marriages. Divorces are plotted in this room and violent plans are schemed. The more time you spend in this place, the more your heart devalues your spouse. It begins the moment you walk in the door, and your care for them lessens with every second that ticks by.

You may say, "But these things are *true!*" Yes, but so are the things in the Appreciation Room. Everyone fails and has areas that need growth. Everyone has unresolved issues, hurts, and personal baggage. This is a sad aspect of being human. We have all sinned. But we have this unfortunate tendency to downplay our own negative attributes while putting our partner's failures under a magnifying glass.

Let's get down to the real issue here. Love

knows about the Depreciation Room and does not live in denial that it exists.

But love chooses not to live there.

You must decide to stop running to this room and lingering there after every frustrating event in your relationship. It does you no good and drains the joy out of your marriage.

Love chooses to believe the best about people. It gives them the benefit of the doubt. It refuses to fill in the unknowns with negative assumptions. And when our worst hopes are proven to be true, love makes every effort to deal with them and move forward. As much as possible, love focuses on the positive.

It's time to start thinking differently. It's time to let love lead your thoughts and your focus. The only reason you should glance in the door of the Depreciation Room is to know how to pray for your spouse. And the only reason you should ever go in this room is to write "COVERED IN LOVE" in huge letters across the walls.

It's time to move into the Appreciation Room, to settle down and make it your home. As you choose to meditate on the positives, you will learn that many more wonderful character qualities could be written across these walls. Your spouse is a living, breathing, endless book to be read. Dreams and hopes have yet to be realized. Talents and abilities may be discovered like hidden treasure. But the choice to explore them starts with a decision by you.

You must develop the habit of reining in your negative thoughts and focusing on the positive attributes of your mate. This is a crucial step as you learn to lead your heart to truly love your spouse. It is a decision that you make, whether they deserve it or not.

## TODAY'S DARE

FOR TODAY'S DARE, GET TWO SHEETS OF PAPER. ON THE FIRST ONE, SPEND A FEW MINUTES WRITING OUT POSITIVE THINGS ABOUT YOUR SPOUSE. THEN DO THE SAME WITH NEGATIVE THINGS ON THE SECOND SHEET. PLACE BOTH SHEETS IN A SECRET PLACE FOR ANOTHER DAY. THERE IS A DIFFERENT PURPOSE AND PLAN FOR EACH. AT SOME POINT DURING THE REMAINDER OF THE DAY, PICK A POSITIVE ATTRIBUTE FROM THE FIRST LIST AND THANK YOUR SPOUSE FOR HAVING THIS CHARACTERISTIC.

\_\_ Check here when you've completed today's dare.

Which list was easier to make? What did this reveal about your thoughts? What attribute did you thank your spouse for having?

_____

_____

_____

_____

_____

_____

_____

_____

_____

_____

_____

_____

_____

_____

_____

_____

*If there is anything praiseworthy —*
*meditate on these things.*
*(Philippians 4:8 NKJV)*

# Day 8
## Love is Not Jealous

Love is as strong as death, its jealousy
unyielding as the grave. It burns like
blazing fire. — Song of Solomon 8:6 NIV

Jealousy is one of the strongest drives
known to man. It comes from the root word
for *zeal* and means "to burn with an intense
fire." The Scripture pointedly says, "Wrath
is fierce and anger is a flood, but who can
stand before jealousy?" (Proverbs 27:4).

There are actually two forms: a *legitimate*
jealousy based upon love, and an *illegitimate*
jealousy based upon envy. Legitimate jealousy sparks when someone you love, who
belongs to you, turns his or her heart away
and replaces you with someone else. If a
wife has an affair and gives herself to
another person, her husband may have a
justified, jealous anger because of his love
for her. He is longing to have back what is
rightfully his.

67

The Bible describes God as having this kind of righteous jealousy for His people. It's not that He is envious *of* us, wishing He had what we have (since He already owns everything). It's that He deeply *longs* for us, desiring for us to keep Him as our first love. He doesn't want us to let anything take precedence over Him in our hearts. The Bible warns us not to worship anything but Him because "the Lord your God is a consuming fire, a jealous God" (Deuteronomy 4:24).

With this established, we will shift our focus to the illegitimate kind of jealousy that is in opposition to love — the one that is rooted in selfishness. This is to be jealous *of* someone, to be "moved with envy."

Do you struggle with being jealous of others? Your friend is more popular, so you feel hatred towards her. Your coworker gets the promotion, so you can't sleep that night. He may have done nothing wrong, but you became bitter because of his success. It has been said that people are fine with your succeeding, just as long as it is not more than theirs.

Jealousy is a common struggle. It is sparked when someone else upstages you and gets something you want. This can be very painful depending upon how selfish you are. Instead of congratulating them, you fume in anger and think ill of them. If you're not careful, jealousy slithers like a viper into your heart and strikes your motivations and relationships. It can poison you from living the life of love God intended.

If you don't diffuse your anger by learning to love others, you may eventually begin plotting against them. The Bible says that envy leads to fighting, quarreling, and every evil thing (James 3:16, 4:1–2).

There is a string of violent jealousy seen throughout Scripture. It caused the first murder when Cain despised God's acceptance of his brother's offering. Sarah sent away her hand-maiden because Hagar could bear children while Sarah could not. Joseph's brothers saw he was their father's favorite, so they threw him in a pit and sold him as a slave. Jesus was more loving, powerful, and popular than the chief priests, so they envied Him and plotted His betrayal and crucifixion.

You don't usually get jealous of disconnected strangers. The ones you're tempted to be jealous of are primarily in the same arena with you. They work in your office, play in your league, run in your circles . . . or live in your house. Yes, if you aren't careful, jealousy can also infect your marriage.

When you were married, you were given the role of becoming your spouse's biggest cheerleader and the captain of his or her fan club. Both of you became one and were to share in the enjoyment of the other. But if selfishness rules, any good thing happening to only one of you can be a catalyst for envy rather than congratulations.

He may be enjoying golf on the weekend while she stays home cleaning the house. He boasts to her about shooting a great score and she feels like shooting *him*.

Or perhaps she is constantly invited to go out with friends while he is left home with the dog. If he's not careful, he can resent her popularity.

Because love is not selfish and puts others first, it refuses to let jealousy in. It leads you to celebrate the successes of your spouse rather than resenting them. A loving husband doesn't mind his wife being better at something, having more fun, or getting more applause. He sees her as completing him, not competing with him.

When he receives praise, he publicly thanks her for her support in aiding his own success. He refuses to brag in such a way that may cause her to resent him. A loving wife will be the first to cheer for her man when he wins. She does not compare her weaknesses to his strengths. She throws a celebration, not a pity party.

It is time to let love, humility, and gratefulness destroy any jealousy that springs up in your heart. It's time to let your mate's successes draw you closer together and give you greater opportunities to show genuine love.

## TODAY'S DARE

DETERMINE TO BECOME YOUR SPOUSE'S BIGGEST FAN AND TO REJECT ANY THOUGHTS OF JEALOUSY. TO HELP YOU SET YOUR HEART ON YOUR SPOUSE AND FOCUS ON THEIR ACHIEVEMENTS, TAKE YESTERDAY'S LIST OF NEGATIVE AT-TRIBUTES AND DISCREETLY BURN IT. THEN SHARE WITH YOUR SPOUSE HOW GLAD YOU ARE ABOUT A SUCCESS HE OR SHE RECENTLY ENJOYED.

__ Check here when you've completed today's dare.

How hard was it to destroy the list? What are some positive experiences that you can celebrate in the life of your mate? How can you encourage them toward future suc-cesses?

_____

_____

_____

_____

_____

_Rejoice with those who rejoice, and weep with those who weep. (Romans 12:15)_

# DAY 9
## LOVE MAKES GOOD
### IMPRESSIONS

Greet one another with a kiss of love.
— 1 Peter 5:14

You've covered some serious ground so far in this journey. Learning to demonstrate aspects of love like patience, kindness, and encouragement are not always easy but are certainly crucial to a healthy relationship. So dealing with the way you greet your spouse each day may seem inconsequential, but this small issue carries surprising significance.

You can tell a lot about the state of a couple's relationship from the way they greet one another. You can see it in their expression and countenance, as well as how they speak to each other. It is even more obvious by their physical contact. But how much importance should you give a greeting?

The Bible has more to say about greetings

75

than you might expect. The apostle Paul took time to encourage his readers to greet one another warmly when they met. In fact, near the end of his letter to the Romans, he asked fellow believers to greet twenty-seven of his friends and loved ones for him. He even took time to list each one by name.

It's not just about your friends, however. Jesus noted in His Sermon on the Mount that even pagans speak kindly to people they like. That's easy for anyone to do. But He took it a step further and said that being godly included being humble and gracious enough to address even your enemies with kindness.

This raises an interesting question. How do you greet your friends, coworkers, and neighbors? How about acquaintances and those you meet in public?

You may even encounter someone you don't necessarily like yet still acknowledge them out of courtesy. So if you're this nice and polite to other people, doesn't your spouse deserve the same? Times ten?

It's probably something you don't think about very often — the first thing you say to him or to her when you wake up in the morning, the look on your face when you get in the car, the energy in your voice when you speak on the telephone. But here's something else you probably don't stop to consider — the difference it would make in your spouse's day if everything about you expressed the fact that you were really, really glad to see them.

When someone communicates that they are glad to see you, your personal sense of self-worth increases. You feel more important and valued. That's because a good greeting sets the stage for positive and healthy interaction. Like love, it puts wind in your sails.

Think back to the story Jesus told of the prodigal son. This young, rebellious man demanded his inheritance money and then wasted it on a foolish lifestyle. But soon his bad choices caught up with him, and he found himself eating scraps in a pigpen. Humbled and ashamed, he practiced his apologies and tried to think of the best way to go home and face his father. But the greeting he was expecting was not the one he received. "While he was still a long way off, his father saw him and felt compassion for him, and ran and embraced him and kissed him" (Luke 15:20).

Of all the scenarios this young man had played out in his mind, this was likely the last one he expected. But how do you think it made him feel to receive his father's embrace and hear his thankful tone? He no doubt felt loved and treasured once again. What do you think it did in their relationship?

What kind of greetings would make your mate feel like that? How could you excite his or her various senses with a simple word, a touch, a tone of voice? A loving greeting can bless your spouse through what they see, hear, and feel.

Think of the opportunities you have to greet each other on a regular basis. When coming through the door. When meeting for lunch. When saying good-night. When talking on the phone.

It doesn't have to be bold and dramatic every time. But adding warmth and enthusiasm gives you the chance to touch your mate's heart in subtle, unspoken ways.

Think about your greeting. Do you use it well? Does your spouse feel valued and appreciated? Do they feel loved? Even when you're not getting along too well, you can lessen the tension and give them value by the way you greet them.

Remember, love is a choice. So choose to change your greeting. Choose to love.

## TODAY'S DARE

THINK OF A SPECIFIC WAY YOU'D LIKE
TO GREET YOUR SPOUSE TODAY. DO IT
WITH A SMILE AND WITH ENTHUSIASM.
THEN DETERMINE TO CHANGE YOUR
GREETING TO REFLECT YOUR LOVE
FOR THEM.

__ Check here when you've completed
today's dare.

When and where did you choose to do your
special greeting? How will you change your
greeting from this point on?

_____

_____

_____

_____

_____

_____

_____

_____

_____

_____

_____

_____

_____

_____

_____

_____

_____

_____

_____

_____

_____

*For I have come to have much joy and comfort in your love. (Philemon 7)*

# Day 10
## Love is
### UNCONDITIONAL

God demonstrates His own love toward
us, in that while we were yet sinners,
Christ died for us. — Romans 5:8

If someone were to ask you, "Why do you
love your wife?" or "Why do you love your
husband?" — what would you say?

Most men would mention their wife's
beauty, her sense of humor, her kindness,
her inner strength. They might talk about
her cooking, her knack for decorating, or
what a good mother she is.

Women would probably say something
about their husband's good looks or his
personality. They'd commend him for his
steadiness and consistent character. They'd
say they love him because he's always there
for them. He's generous. He's helpful.

But what if over the course of years, your
wife or husband stopped being every one of
these things. Would you still love them?

Based on your answers above, the only logical response would be "no." If your reasons for loving your spouse all have something to do with his or her qualities — and then those same qualities suddenly or gradually disappear — your basis for love is over.

The only way love can last a lifetime is if it's unconditional. The truth is this: love is not determined by the one *being* loved but rather by the one *choosing* to love.

The Bible refers to this kind of love by using the Greek word *agape* (pronounced *uh-GOP-ay*).

It differs from the other types of love, which are — *phileo* (friendship) and *eros* (sexual love). Both friendship and sex have an important place in marriage, of course, and are definitely part of the house you build together as husband and wife. But if your marriage totally depends on having common interests or enjoying a healthy sex life, then the foundation of your relationship is unstable.

*Phileo* and *eros* are more responsive in nature and can fluctuate based upon feelings. *Agape* love, on the other hand, is selfless and unconditional. So unless this kind of love forms the foundation of your marriage, the wear and tear of time will destroy it. *Agape* love is "in sickness and health" love, "for richer or poorer" love, "for better or worse" love. It is the only kind of love that is *true* love.

That's because this is God's kind of love. He doesn't love us because we are lovable but because He is so loving. The Bible says, "In this is love, not that we loved God, but that He loved us and sent His Son to be the propitiation for our sins" (1 John 4:10). If He insisted that we prove ourselves worthy of His love, we would fail miserably. But God's love is a choice He makes completely on His own. It's something we receive from Him and then share with others. "We love, because He first loved us" (1 John 4:19).

If a man says to his wife, "I have fallen out of love with you," he is actually saying, "I never loved you unconditionally to begin with." His love was based on feelings or circumstances rather than commitment. That's the result of building a marriage on *phileo* or *eros* love. There must be a stronger foundation than mere friendship or sexual attraction. Unconditional love, *agape* love, will not be swayed by time or circumstance.

That's not to say, though, that love which began for the wrong reasons cannot be restored and redeemed. In fact, when you rebuild your marriage with *agape* as its foundation, then the friendship and romantic aspects of your love become more endearing than ever before. When your enjoyment of each other as best friends and lovers is based on unwavering commitment, you will experience an intimacy that cannot be achieved any other way.

But you will struggle and fail to attain this kind of marriage unless you allow God to begin growing His love within you. Love that "bears all things, believes all things, hopes all things, endures all things" (1 Corinthians 13:7) does not come from within. It can only come from God.

The Scriptures say that "neither death, nor life, nor angels, nor principalities, nor things present, nor things to come, nor powers, nor height, nor depth, nor any other created thing, will be able to separate us from the love of God, which is in Christ Jesus our Lord" (Romans 8:38–39). This is God's kind of love. And thankfully — by your choice — it can become *your* kind of love. But first you must receive it and share it.

And don't be surprised, when your spouse begins living confidently under its shade, if he or she doesn't become even more lovable to you than you remember. You will no longer say, "I love you because . . ." You will now say, "I love you, period."

## TODAY'S DARE

DO SOMETHING OUT OF THE ORDINARY TODAY FOR YOUR SPOUSE — SOMETHING THAT PROVES (TO YOU AND TO THEM) THAT YOUR LOVE IS BASED ON YOUR CHOICE AND NOTHING ELSE. WASH HER CAR. CLEAN THE KITCHEN. BUY HIS FAVORITE DESSERT. FOLD THE LAUNDRY. DEMONSTRATE LOVE TO THEM FOR THE SHEER JOY OF BEING THEIR PARTNER IN MARRIAGE.

__ Check here when you've completed today's dare.

Has your love in the past been based on your spouse's attributes and behavior, or on your commitment? How can you continue to show love when it's not returned in a way you hoped for?

_____

_____

_____

_____

_____

_He who trusts in the Lord, lovingkindness
shall surround him. (Psalm 32:10)_

# DAY 11
## LOVE CHERISHES

Husbands ought also to love their own
wives as their own bodies.
— Ephesians 5:28

Consider these two scenarios.

A man's older car begins having serious trouble, so he takes it to a mechanic. After an assessment is made, he is told it will need a complete overhaul, which would tax his limited budget. Because of the expensive repairs, he determines to get rid of the car and spend his funds on a new vehicle. Seems reasonable, right?

Another man, an engineer, accidentally crushes his hand in a piece of equipment. He rushes to the hospital and has it x-rayed, finding that numerous bones are broken. Although frustrated and in pain, he willingly uses his savings to have it doctored and placed in a cast, then gingerly nurses it back to health over the following months.

This, too, probably seems reasonable to you.

The problem within our culture is that marriage is more often treated like the first scenario. When your relationship experiences difficulty, you are urged to dump your spouse for a "newer model." But those who have this view do not understand the significant bond between a husband and wife. The truth is, marriage is more like the second scenario. You are a part of one another. You would never cut off your hand if it was injured but would pay whatever you could afford for the best medical treatment possible. That's because your hand is priceless to you. It is part of who you are.

And so is your mate. Marriage is a beautiful mystery created by God, joining two lives together as one. This not only happens physically but spiritually and emotionally. You start off sharing the same house, the same bed, the same last name. Your identity as individuals has been joined into one. When your spouse goes through a tragedy, both of you feel it. When you find success at your job, both of you rejoice. But somewhere along the way, you experience disappointment, and the sobering reality that you married an imperfect person sets in.

This, however, does not change the fact

that your spouse is still a part of you. Ephesians 5:28–29 says, "Husbands ought also to love their own wives as their own bodies. He who loves his own wife loves himself; for no one ever hated his own flesh, but nourishes and cherishes it."

This verse speaks to husbands, but notice how each member is viewed. They are both considered to be the same flesh. You must treat them with the same nurture and care that you treat yourself. When you show love to your spouse, you are showing love to yourself as well.

But there is a flip side to this coin. When you mistreat your mate, you are also mistreating yourself. Think about it. Your lives are now interwoven together. Your spouse cannot experience joy or pain, blessing or cursing, without it also affecting you. So when you attack your mate, it is like attacking your own body.

It's time to let love change your thinking. It's time for you to realize that your spouse is as much a part of you as your hand, your eye, or your heart. She, too, needs to be loved and cherished. And if she has issues causing pain or frustration, then you should care for these with the same love and tenderness as you would a bodily injury. If he is wounded in some way, you should think of yourself as an instrument that helps bring healing to his life.

In light of this, think about how you treat your spouse's physical body. Do you cherish it as your own? Do you treat it with respect and tenderness? Do you take pleasure in who they are? Or do you make them feel foolish or embarrassed? Just as you treasure your eyes, hands, and feet, you should treasure your spouse as a priceless gift.

Don't let the culture around you determine the worth of your marriage. To compare it with something that can be discarded or replaced is to dishonor God's purpose for it. That would be like amputating a limb. Instead, it should be a picture of love between two imperfect people who choose to love each other regardless.

Whenever a husband looks into the eyes of his wife, he should remember that "he who loves his wife loves himself." And a wife should remember that when she loves him, she is also giving love and honor to herself.

When you look at your mate, you're looking at a part of *you.* So treat her well. Speak highly of him. Nourish and cherish the love of your life.

## TODAY'S DARE

WHAT NEED DOES YOUR SPOUSE HAVE THAT YOU COULD MEET TODAY? CAN YOU RUN AN ERRAND? GIVE A BACK RUB OR FOOT MASSAGE? IS THERE HOUSEWORK YOU COULD HELP WITH? CHOOSE A GESTURE THAT SAYS, "I CHERISH YOU" AND DO IT WITH A SMILE.

__ Check here when you've completed today's dare.

What did you choose to show that you cherish your mate? What did you learn from this experience?

_____

_____

_____

_____

_____

_____

_____

_Answering him, Jesus said, "What do you want Me to do for you?" (Mark 10:51)_

# DAY 12
## LOVE LETS THE OTHER WIN

Do not merely look out for your own personal interests, but also for the interests of others. — Philippians 2:4

If you were asked to name three areas where you and your spouse disagree, you'd likely be able to do it without thinking very hard. You might even be able to produce a top ten list if given a few more minutes. And sadly, unless someone at your house starts doing some giving in, these same issues are going to keep popping up between you and your mate.

Unfortunately, stubbornness comes as a standard feature on both husband and wife models. Defending your rights and opinions is a foundational part of your nature and make-up. It's detrimental, though, inside a marriage relationship, and it steals away time and productivity. It can also cause great frustration for both of you.

Granted, being stubborn is not always bad. Some things are worth standing up for and protecting. Our priorities, morals, and obedience to God should be guarded with great effort. But too often we debate over piddling things, like the color of wall paint or the choice of restaurants.

Other times, of course, the stakes are much higher. One of you would like more children; the other doesn't. One of you wants to vacation with your extended family; the other doesn't. One of you prefers home-schooling your kids; the other doesn't. One of you thinks it's time for marriage counseling or to get more involved in a church, while the other doesn't.

Though these issues may not crop up every day, they keep resurfacing and don't really go away. You never seem to get any closer to a resolution or compromise. The heels just keep digging in. It's like driving with the parking brake on.

There's only one way to get beyond stalemates like these, and that's by finding a word that's the opposite of *stubbornness* — a word we first met back while discussing kindness. That word is "willing." It's an attitude and spirit of cooperation that should permeate our conversations. It's like a palm tree by the ocean that endures the greatest winds because it knows how to gracefully bend. And the one best example of it is Jesus Christ, as described in Philippians 2. Follow the progression of His selfless love . . .

As God, He had every right to refuse becoming a man but yielded and did — because He was willing. He had the right to be served by all mankind but came to serve us instead. He had the right to live in peace and safety but willingly laid down His life for our sins. He was even willing to endure the grueling torture of the cross. He loved, cooperated, and was willing to do His Father's will instead of His own.

In light of this amazing testimony, the Bible applies to us a one-sentence summary statement: "Have this attitude in yourselves which was also in Christ Jesus" (Philippians 2:5) — the attitude of willingness, flexibility, and humble submission. It means laying down for the good of others what you have the right to claim for yourself.

All it takes for your present arguments to continue is for both of you to stay entrenched and unbending. But the very moment one of you says, "I'm willing to go your way on this one," the argument will be over. And though the follow-through may cost you some pride and discomfort, you have made a loving, lasting investment in your marriage.

"Yes, but then I'll look foolish. I'll lose the fight. I'll lose control." You've already looked foolish by being bullheaded and refusing to listen. You've already lost the fight by making this issue more important than your marriage and your spouse's sense of worth. You may have already lost emotional control by saying things that got personal and hurt your mate.

The wise and loving thing to do is to start approaching your disagreements with a willingness to not always insist on your own way. That's not to say your mate is necessarily right or being wise about a matter, but you are choosing to give strong consideration to their preference as a way of valuing them.

Love's best advice comes from the Bible, which says, "The wisdom that is from above is first pure, then peaceable, gentle, willing to yield" (James 3:17 NKJV). Instead of treating your wife or husband like an enemy or someone to be guarded against, start by treating them as your closest, most honored friend. Give their words full weight.

No, you won't always see eye-to-eye. You're not supposed to be carbon copies of each other. If you were, one of you would be unnecessary. Two people who always share the same opinions and perspectives won't have any balance or flavor to enhance the relationship. Rather, your differences are for listening to and learning from.

Are you willing to bend to demonstrate love to your spouse? Or are you refusing to give in because of pride? If it doesn't matter in the long run — especially in eternity — then give up your rights and choose to honor the one you love. It will be both good for you and good for your marriage.

## TODAY'S DARE

DEMONSTRATE LOVE BY WILLINGLY CHOOSING TO GIVE IN TO AN AREA OF DISAGREEMENT BETWEEN YOU AND YOUR SPOUSE. TELL THEM YOU ARE PUTTING THEIR PREFERENCE FIRST.

__ Check here when you've completed today's dare.

What issue did you choose? What did giving in cost you? How will this help you in the future?

_____

_____

_____

_____

_____

_____

_____

_____

_____

_____

_____

_____

_____

_____

_____

_____

_____

_____

_____

*If possible, so far as it depends on you,
be at peace with all men. (Romans 12:18)*

# Day 13
## Love fights fair

If a house is divided against itself, that
house will not be able to stand.
— Mark 3:25

Like it or not, conflict in marriage is simply
inevitable. When you tied the knot as bride
and groom, you joined not only your hopes
and dreams but also your hurts, fears,
imperfections, and emotional baggage.
From the moment you unpacked from your
honeymoon, you began the real process of
unpacking one another, unpleasantly discovering how sinful and selfish each of you
could be.

Pretty soon your mate started to slip off
your lofty pedestal, and you off of theirs.
The forced closeness of marriage began
stripping away your public façades, exposing your private problems and secret habits.
Welcome to fallen humanity.

At the same time, the storms of life began

testing and revealing what you're really made of. Work demands, health issues, in-law arguments, and financial needs flared up in varying degrees, adding pressure and heat to the relationship. This sets the stage for disagreements to break out between the two of you. You argued and fought. You hurt. You experienced conflict. But you are not alone.

Every couple goes through it. It's par for the course. But not every couple survives it.

So don't think living out today's dare will drive all conflict from your marriage. Instead, this is about dealing with conflict in such a way that you come out healthier on the other side.

Both of you. Together.

The deepest, most heartbreaking damage you'll ever do (or ever have done) to your marriage will most likely occur in the thick of conflict. That's because this is when your pride is strongest. Your anger is hottest. You're the most selfish and judgmental. Your words contain the most venom. You make the worst decisions. A great marriage on Monday can start driving off the cliff on Tuesday if unbridled conflict takes over and neither of you has your foot on the brakes.

But love steps in and changes things. Love reminds you that your marriage is too valuable to allow it to self-destruct, and that your love for your spouse is more important than whatever you're fighting about. Love helps you install air bags and to set up guardrails in your relationship. It reminds you that conflict can actually be turned around for good. Married couples who learn to work through conflict tend to be closer, more trusting, more intimate, and enjoy a much deeper connection afterwards.

But how? The wisest way is to learn to fight clean by establishing healthy rules of engagement. If you don't have guidelines for how you'll approach hot topics, you won't stay in bounds when the action heats up.

Basically there are two types of boundaries for dealing with conflict: "we" boundaries and "me" boundaries.

*"We" boundaries* are rules you both agree on beforehand, rules that apply during any fight or altercation. And each of you has the right to gently but directly enforce them if these rules are violated. These could include:

1. We will never mention divorce.
2. We will not bring up old, unrelated items from the past.

3. We will never fight in public or in front of our children.
4. We will call a "time out" if conflict escalates to a damaging level.
5. We will never touch one another in a harmful way.
6. We will never go to bed angry with one another.
7. Failure is not an option. Whatever it takes, we will work this out.

*"Me" boundaries* are rules you personally practice on your own. Here are some of the most effective examples:

1. I will listen first before speaking. "Everyone must be quick to hear, slow to speak and slow to anger" (James 1:19).
2. I will deal with my own issues up-front. "Why do you look at the speck that is in your brother's eye, but do not notice the log that is in your own eye?" (Matthew 7:3)
3. I will speak gently and keep my voice down. "A gentle answer turns away wrath, but a harsh word stirs up anger" (Proverbs 15:1).

Fighting fair means changing your weapons. Disagreeing with dignity. It should result in building a bridge instead of burning one down. Remember, love is not a fight, but it is always worth fighting for.

## TODAY'S DARE

TALK WITH YOUR SPOUSE ABOUT ESTABLISHING HEALTHY RULES OF ENGAGEMENT. IF YOUR MATE IS NOT READY FOR THIS, THEN WRITE OUT YOUR OWN PERSONAL RULES TO "FIGHT" BY. RESOLVE TO ABIDE BY THEM WHEN THE NEXT DISAGREEMENT OCCURS.

__ Check here when you've completed today's dare.

If your spouse participated with you, what was their response? What rules did you write for yourself?

_____

_____

_____

_____

_____

_____

_____

_____

_____

_____

_____

_____

_____

_____

_____

_____

_____

_____

_____

*Be of the same mind toward one another.*
*(Romans 12:16)*

# Day 14
## Love takes delight

Enjoy life with the wife you love all the
days of your fleeting life.
— Ecclesiastes 9:9 HCSB

One of the most important things you should learn on your Love Dare journey is that you should not just *follow* your heart. You should *lead* it. You don't let your feelings and emotions do the driving. You put them in the back seat and tell them where you're going.

In your marriage relationship, you won't always feel like loving. It is unrealistic for your heart to constantly thrill at the thought of spending every moment with your spouse. Nobody can maintain a burning desire for togetherness just on feelings alone. But it's also difficult to love someone only out of obligation.

A newlywed takes delight in the one they now call their spouse. Their love is fresh and young, and the hopes for a romantic future linger in their hearts. However, there is something just as powerful as that fresh, new love. It comes from the *decision* to delight in your spouse and to love him or her no matter how long you've been married. In other words, love that *chooses* to love is just as powerful as love that *feels* like loving. In many ways, it's a truer love because it has its eyes wide open.

Left to ourselves, we'll always lean toward being disapproving of one another. She'll get on your nerves. He'll aggravate you. But our days are too short to waste in bickering over petty things. Life is too fleeting for that.

Instead, it's time to lead your heart to once again delight in your mate. *Enjoy* your spouse. Take her hand and seek her companionship. Desire his conversation. Remember why you fell in love with her personality. Accept this person — quirks and all — and welcome him or her back into your heart.

Again, you get to choose what you treasure. It's not like you're born with certain pre-sets and preferences you're destined to operate from. If you're irritable, it's because you choose to be. If you can't function without a clean house, it's because you've decided no other way will do. If you pick at your mate more than you praise them, it's because you've allowed your heart to be selfish. You've led yourself into criticism.

So now it's time to lead your heart back out. It's time to learn to delight in your spouse again, then to watch your heart actually start enjoying who they are.

It may surprise you to know that the Bible contains many romantic love stories, none more blatant and provocative than all eight chapters from the Song of Solomon. Listen to the way these two lovers take pleasure in one another in this poetic book . . .

The woman: "Like an apple tree among the trees of the forest, so is my beloved among the young men. In his shade I took great delight and sat down, and his fruit was sweet to my taste. He has brought me to his banquet hall, and his banner over me is love" (Song of Solomon 2:3–4).

The man: "Arise, my darling, my beautiful one, and come along! O my dove, in the clefts of the rock, in the secret place of the steep pathway, let me see your form, let me hear your voice; for your voice is sweet, and your form is lovely" (Song of Solomon 2:13–14).

Too sappy? Too mushy? Not for those who lead their heart to delight in their beloved — even when the new wears off, even when she's wearing rollers in her hair, even when his hair is falling out. It's time to remember why you once fell in love. To laugh again. To flirt again. To dream again. Delightfully.

Today's dare may be directing you to a real and radical change of heart. For some, the move toward delight may be only a small step away. For others, it may require a giant leap from ongoing disgust.

But if you've been delighted before — which you were when you got married — you can be delighted again. Even if it's been a long time. Even if a whole lot has happened to change your perceptions.

The responsibility is yours to relearn what you love about this one to whom you've promised yourself forever.

## TODAY'S DARE

PURPOSEFULLY NEGLECT AN ACTIVITY YOU WOULD NORMALLY DO SO YOU CAN SPEND QUALITY TIME WITH YOUR SPOUSE. DO SOMETHING HE OR SHE WOULD LOVE TO DO OR A PROJECT THEY'D REALLY LIKE TO WORK ON. JUST BE TOGETHER.

__ Check here when you've completed today's dare.

What did you decide to give up? What did you do together? How did it go? What new thing did you learn (or relearn) about your spouse?

_____

_____

_____

_____

_____

_____

_____

_____

_____

_____

_____

_____

_____

_____

_____

_____

*To find out more about "leading your heart," see Appendix IV*

*Give me your heart . . . and let your eyes delight in my ways. (Proverbs 23:26)*

# DAY 15
## LOVE IS HONORABLE

Live with your wives in an understanding way . . . and show her honor as a fellow heir of the grace of life. — 1 Peter 3:7

There are certain words in our language that have powerful meanings. Whenever these words are used, an air of respect is associated with them. These words never lose their timeless quality, class, and dignity. One of these will be our focus for today. It is the word *honor.*

To honor someone means to give them respect and high esteem, to treat them as being special and of great worth. When you speak to them, you keep your language clean and understandable. You are courteous and polite. When they speak to you, you take them seriously, giving their words weight and significance. When they ask you to do something, you accommodate them if at all possible, simply out of respect for who they are.

The Bible tells us to "honor" our father and mother, as well as those in authority. It is a call to acknowledge the position or value of someone else. *Honor* is a noble word.

This is especially true in marriage. Honoring your mate means giving him or her your full attention, not talking to them from behind a newspaper or with one eye on the television. When decisions are being made that affect both of you or your whole family, you give your mate's voice and opinion equal influence in your mind. You honor what they have to say. They matter — and because of the way you treat them, they should know it.

But there's another word that calls us to a higher place, a word that isn't often equated with marriage, though its relevance cannot be understated. It's a word that actually forms the basis for honor — the very reason why we give respect and high regard to our husband or wife. That word is *holy.*

To say your mate should be "holy" to you doesn't mean that he or she is perfect. Holiness means they are set apart for a higher purpose — no longer common or everyday but special and unique. A person who has become holy to you has a place no one can rival in your heart. He or she is sacred to you, a person to be honored, praised, and defended.

A bride treats her wedding dress this way. After wearing it on her special day, she covers and protects it, then sets it apart from everything else in her closet. You won't catch her in it when she's working in the yard or going out on the town. Her wedding dress has a value all its own. In this way, it is holy and sacred to her.

When two people marry, each spouse becomes "holy" to each other by way of "holy matrimony." This means no other person in the whole world is supposed to enjoy this level of commitment and endearment from you. Your relationship is like no other. You share physical intimacy with only her, only him. You establish a home with this person. You bear your children with this person. Your heart, your possessions, your life itself is to be wrapped up in the uncommon bond you share with this one individual.

Is that the way it is in your marriage? Would your mate say you honor and respect them? Do you consider them set apart and highly valued? Holy?

Perhaps you *don't* feel this way, and maybe for good reason. Perhaps you wish some outsider could see the level of disrespect you get from your wife or husband — someone who would make your mate feel embarrassed to be exposed for who they really are behind closed doors.

But that's not the issue with love. Love honors even when it's rejected. Love treats its beloved as special and sacred even when an ungrateful attitude is all you get in return.

It's marvelous, of course, when a husband and wife are joined in this purpose, when they're following the biblical command to be "devoted to one another" in love, when they're giving "preference to one another in honor" (Romans 12:10). "Marriage should be honored by all, and the marriage bed kept pure" (Hebrews 13:4 NIV).

But when your attempts at honor go un-reciprocated, you are to give honor just the same. That's what love dares to do — to say, "Of all the relationships I have, I will value ours the most. Of all the things I'm willing to sacrifice, I will sacrifice the most for you. With all your failures, sins, mistakes, and faults — past and present — I still choose to love and honor you." That's how you create an atmosphere for love to be rekindled. That's how you lead your heart to truly love your mate again. And that's the beauty of honor.

## TODAY'S DARE

CHOOSE A WAY TO SHOW HONOR AND RESPECT TO YOUR SPOUSE THAT IS ABOVE YOUR NORMAL ROUTINE. IT MAY BE HOLDING THE DOOR FOR HER. IT MIGHT BE PUTTING HIS CLOTHES AWAY FOR HIM. IT MAY BE THE WAY YOU LISTEN AND SPEAK IN YOUR COMMUNICATION. SHOW YOUR MATE THAT HE OR SHE IS HIGHLY ESTEEMED IN YOUR EYES.

__ Check here when you've completed today's dare.

How did you choose to show honor? What was the result? What are some other ways you could demonstrate honor in the coming days?

_____

_____

_____

_____

_____

_____

_____

_____

_____

_____

_____

_____

_____

_____

_____

_____

_____

_____

*I will also honor them and they will not be insignificant. (Jeremiah 30:19)*

# DAY 16
## LOVE INTERCEDES

Beloved, I pray that in all respects you may prosper and be in good health, just as your soul prospers. — 3 John 2

You cannot change your spouse. As much as you may want to, you cannot play God and reach into their heart and mold them into what you want them to be. But that's what most couples spend a large part of their time trying to do — change their spouse.

Insanity has been described as doing the same thing over and over and expecting different results. But isn't that what happens when you try to change your mate? It's frustration at the highest level. At some point you have to accept that it's not something you can do. But here's what you *can* do. You can become a "wise farmer."

A farmer cannot make a seed grow into a fruitful crop. He cannot argue, manipulate, or demand it to bear fruit. But he can plant the seed into fertile soil, give it water and nutrients, protect it from weeds, and then turn it over to God. Millions of farmers have made a livelihood from this process over the centuries. They know that not every seed sprouts. But most *will* grow when planted in proper soil and given what they need.

There is no guarantee that anything in this book will change your spouse. But that's not what this book is about. It's about you daring to love. If you take the Love Dare seriously, there is a high likelihood that you will be personally changed from the inside out.

And if you carry out each dare, your spouse will likely be affected and your marriage will begin to bloom in front of your eyes. It may take weeks. It may even take years. But regardless of the soil you're working with, you are to plan for success. You are to get the weeds out of your marriage. You are to nurture the soil of your mate's heart and then depend on God for the results.

But you won't be able to do this alone. You will need something that is more powerful than anything else you have. And that is effective prayer.

Prayer really does work. It's a spiritual phenomenon created by an unlimited, powerful God. And it yields amazing results.

Do you feel like giving up on your marriage? Jesus said to pray instead of quitting (Luke 18:1). Are you stressed out and worried? Prayer can bring peace to your storms (Philippians 4:6–7) Do you need a major breakthrough? Prayer can make the difference (Acts 12:1–17).

God is sovereign. He does things His way. He's not a genie in a lamp that submits to your every wish. But He does love you and desires an intimate relationship with you. This doesn't happen apart from prayer.

There are some key elements that must be in place for prayer to be effective. But suffice it to say that prayer works best when coming from a humble heart that is in a right relationship with God and others. The Bible says, "Confess your sins to one another, and pray for one another. . . . The effective prayer of a righteous man can accomplish much" (James 5:16).

Have you ever wondered why God gives you overwhelming insight into your spouse's hidden faults? Do you really think it's for endless nagging? No, it is for effective kneeling. No one knows better how to pray for your mate than you.

Has your scolding or nagging been working? The answer is no, because that's not what changes a heart. It is time to try talking to God in your prayer closet instead.

A husband will find that God can "fix" his wife a lot better than he can. A wife will accomplish more through strategic prayer than from all her persuasive efforts. It is also a much more pleasant way to live.

So turn your complaints into prayers and watch the Master work while you keep your hands clean. If your spouse doesn't have any type of relationship with God, then it's clear what you need to start praying for.

Beyond this, begin to pray for exactly what your mate needs. Pray for his heart. Pray for her attitude. Pray for your spouse's responsibilities before God. Pray for truth to replace lies. Pray that forgiveness would replace bitterness. Pray for a genuine breakthrough in your marriage. And then pray for your heart's desires — for love and honor to become the norm. Pray for romance and intimacy to go to a deeper level.

One of the most loving things you can ever do for your spouse is to pray for them. "Ask, and it will be given to you; seek, and you will find; knock, and it will be opened to you" (Matthew 7:7).

## TODAY'S DARE

BEGIN PRAYING TODAY FOR YOUR SPOUSE'S HEART. PRAY FOR THREE SPECIFIC AREAS WHERE YOU DESIRE FOR GOD TO WORK IN YOUR SPOUSE'S LIFE AND IN YOUR MARRIAGE.

__ Check here when you've completed today's dare.

Have you experienced the power of prayer in the past? What did you choose to pray about? Was it easy for you, or did it feel foreign to you?

_____

_____

_____

_____

_____

_____

_____

_____

_____

_____

_____

_____

_____

_____

_____

_____

_____

*For insight into the keys of effective
prayer, see Appendix I*

*If anyone is God-fearing and does His
will, He listens to him. (John 9:31)*

# DAY 17
## LOVE PROMOTES
### INTIMACY

---

He who covers over an offense promotes
love, but whoever repeats the matter
separates close friends.
— Proverbs 17:9 NIV

You can be close to a good friend you've
known since childhood or college days. You
can be close to a sibling, your parents, or a
cousin who's about your same age. But
nothing rivals the closeness that's experienced between a husband and wife. Marriage is the most intimate of all human
relationships.

That's why we need it so much. Each of
us comes into life with an inborn hunger to
be known, loved, and accepted. We want
people to know our name, to recognize us
when they see us, and to value who we are.
The prospect of sharing our home with
another person who knows us down to the
most intimate detail is part of the deep

pleasure of marriage.

Yet this great blessing is also the site of its greatest danger. Someone who knows us this intimately can either love us at depths we never imagined, or can wound us in ways we may never fully recover from. It's both the fire and the fear of marriage.

Which of these are you experiencing the most in your home right now? Are the secrets your spouse knows about you reasons for *shame,* or reasons for drawing you *closer?* If your spouse were to answer this same question, would they say you make them feel *safe,* or *scared?*

If home is not considered a place of safety, you will both be tempted to seek it somewhere else. Perhaps you might look to another person, initiating a relationship that either flirts with adultery or actually enters in. You may look for comfort in work or in outside hobbies, something that partially shields you from intimacy but also keeps you around people who respect and accept you.

Your mate should not feel pressured to be perfect in order to receive your approval. They should not walk on eggshells in the very place where they ought to feel the most comfortable in their bare feet. The Bible says, "There is no fear in love; but perfect love casts out fear" (1 John 4:18). The atmosphere in your marriage should be one of freedom. Like Adam and Eve in the garden, your closeness should only intensify your intimacy. Being "naked" and "not ashamed" (Genesis 2:25) should exist in the same sentence, right in your marriage — physically and emotionally.

Admittedly, this is tender territory. Marriage has unloaded another person's baggage into your life, and yours into theirs. Both of you have reason to feel embarrassed that this much has been revealed about you to another living soul. But this is your opportunity to wrap all this private information about them in the protective embrace of your love, and promise to be the one who can best help him or her deal with it.

*Some of these secrets may need correcting.* Therefore, you can be an agent of healing and repair — not by lecturing, not by criticizing, but by listening in love and offering support.

*Some of these secrets just need to be accepted.* They are part of this person's make-up and history. And though these issues may not be very pleasant to deal with, they will always require a gentle touch.

In either case, you and you alone wield the power either to reject your spouse because of this or to welcome them in — warts and all. They will either know they're in a place of safety where they are free to make mistakes, or they will recoil into themselves and be lost to you, perhaps forever. Loving them well should be your life's work.

Think of it this way. No one knows you better than God does, the One who made you. The writer of Psalm 139 was right when he said, "You know when I sit down and when I rise up; You understand my thought from afar. You scrutinize my path and my lying down, and are intimately acquainted with all my ways. Even before there is a word on my tongue, behold, O Lord, You know it all" (Psalm 139:2–4).

And yet God, who knows secrets about us that we even hide from ourselves, loves us at a depth we cannot begin to fathom. How much more should we — as imperfect people — reach out to our spouse in grace and understanding, accepting them for who they are and assuring them that their secrets are safe with us?

This may be an area where you've really failed in the past. If so, don't expect your mate to immediately give you wide-open access to their heart. You must begin to rebuild trust. Jesus Himself is described as

One who doesn't barge into people's lives but who stands at the door and knocks. "If anyone hears My voice and opens the door, I will come in to him and will dine with him, and he with Me" (Revelation 3:20).

The reality of intimacy always takes time to develop, especially after being compromised. But your commitment to re-establishing it can happen today — for anyone willing to take the dare.

## Today's Dare

Determine to guard your mate's secrets (unless they are dangerous to them or to you) and to pray for them. Talk with your spouse, and resolve to demonstrate love in spite of these issues. Really listen to them when they share personal thoughts and struggles with you. Make them feel safe.

__ Check here when you've completed today's dare.

How much of an effort is it for you to hold back from saying something, critical or otherwise? What have you learned about your spouse today, simply from listening?

_____

_____

_____

_____

_____

_I am my beloved's and my beloved is mine. (Song of Solomon 6:3)_

# DAY 18
## LOVE SEEKS TO UNDERSTAND

How blessed is the man who finds
wisdom, and the man who gains
understanding. — Proverbs 3:13

We enjoy discovering as much as we can about the things we truly care about. If it's our favorite football team, we'll read any article that helps us keep up with how they're doing. If it's cooking, we'll tune to those channels that share the best grilling techniques or dessert recipes. If there's a subject that appeals to us, we'll take notice any time it comes up. In fact, it's often like an area of personal study.

It's fine, of course, to have outside interests and to be knowledgeable about certain things. But this is where love would ask the question, "How much do you know about your mate?"

Think back to the days when you were courting. Didn't you study the one your heart was yearning for?

When a man is trying to win the heart of a woman, he studies her. He learns her likes, dislikes, habits, and hobbies. But after he wins her heart and marries her, he often stops learning about her. The mystery and challenge of knowing her seems less intriguing, and he finds his interests drifting to other areas.

This is also true in many cases for women, who start off admiring and building respect for the man they desire to be with. But after marriage, those feelings begin to fade as reality reveals that her "prince" is a flawed and imperfect man.

Yet there are still hidden things to discover about your spouse. And this understanding will help draw you closer together. It can even give you favor in the eyes of your mate. "Good understanding produces favor" (Proverbs 13:15).

Consider the following perspective: if the amount you studied your spouse before marriage were equal to a high school diploma, then you should continue to learn about your mate until you gain a "college degree," a "master's degree," and ultimately a "doctorate degree." Think of it as a lifelong journey that draws your heart ever closer to your mate.

- Do you know his or her greatest hopes and dreams?
- Do you fully understand how they prefer to give and receive love?
- Do you know what your spouse's greatest fears are and why they struggle with them?

Some of the problems you have in relating to your spouse are simply because you don't understand them. They probably react very differently to certain situations than you do, and you can't figure out why.

These differences — even the ones that are relatively insignificant — can be the cause of many fights and conflicts in your marriage. That's because, as the Bible says, we tend to "revile" those things we don't understand (Jude 10).

There are reasons for his or her tastes and preferences. Each nuance in your spouse's character has a back story. Each element of who he is, how he thinks, and what he's like is couched in a set of guiding principles, which often makes sense only to the person who holds them. But it's worth the time it will take to study why they are the way they are.

If you miss the level of intimacy you once shared with your spouse, one of the best ways to unlock their heart again is by making a commitment to know them. Study them. Read them like a book you're trying to understand.

*Ask questions.* The Bible says, "The ear of the wise seeks knowledge" (Proverbs 18:15). Love takes the initiative to begin conversations. In order to get your mate to open up, they need to know that your desire for understanding them is real and genuine.

*Listen.* "Wise men store up knowledge, but with the mouth of the foolish, ruin is at hand" (Proverbs 10:14). The goal of understanding your mate is to hear them, not to tell them what you think. Even if your spouse is not very talkative, love calls you to draw out the "deep water" that dwells within them (Proverbs 20:5).

*Ask God for discernment.* "The Lord gives wisdom; from His mouth come knowledge and understanding" (Proverbs 2:6). Things like gender differences, family backgrounds, and varied life experiences can cloud your ability to know your mate's heart and motivations. But God is a giver of wisdom. The Lord will show you what you need in order to know how to love your spouse better.

"By wisdom a house is built, and by understanding it is established; and by knowledge the rooms are filled with all precious and pleasant riches" (Proverbs 24:3–4). There is a depth of beauty and meaning inside your wife or husband that will amaze you as you discover more of it. Enter the mystery with expectation and enthusiasm. Desire to know this person even better than you do now. Make him or her your chosen field of study, and you will fill your home with the kind of riches only love can provide.

## TODAY'S DARE

PREPARE A SPECIAL DINNER AT HOME, JUST FOR THE TWO OF YOU. THE DINNER CAN BE AS NICE AS YOU PREFER. FOCUS THIS TIME ON GETTING TO KNOW YOUR SPOUSE BETTER, PERHAPS IN AREAS YOU'VE RARELY TALKED ABOUT. DETERMINE TO MAKE IT AN ENJOYABLE EVENING FOR YOU AND YOUR MATE.

___ Check here when you've completed today's dare.

What did you learn about your spouse that you didn't know before? How could you continue this process of discovery in other ways, at other times? What were some of the moments that made this evening memorable?

_____

_____

_____

_____

_____

_____

_____

_____

_____

_____

_____

_____

_____

_____

_____

*For a list of questions related to today's
dare, see Appendix II*

*Acquire wisdom; and with all your
acquiring, get understanding.
(Proverbs 4:7)*

# DAY 19
## LOVE IS IMPOSSIBLE

Let us love one another, for love is from God; and everyone who loves is born of God and knows God. — 1 John 4:7

The Love Dare starts with a secret. And though it's been an unspoken element throughout each day, you've likely grown more and more suspicious of it all the time. Now that you're this far, it's a secret you're discovering for yourself, even if you haven't exactly known how to put it into words.

The secret is this: you cannot manufacture unconditional love (or *agape* love) out of your own heart. It's impossible. It's beyond your capabilities. It's beyond *all* our capabilities.

You may have demonstrated kindness and unselfishness in some form, and you may have learned to be more thoughtful and considerate. But sincerely loving someone unselfishly and unconditionally is another matter altogether.

So how can you do it? Like it or not, *agape* love isn't something you *can* do. It's something only God can do. But because of His great love for you — and His love for your spouse — He chooses to express His love *through* you.

Still, you may not believe that. You may be convinced that with enough hard work and commitment, you can muster up unconditional, long-term, sacrificial love from your own heart. You want to believe it's in you.

But how many times has your love failed to keep you from lying, from lusting, from overreacting, from thinking evil of this person you've vowed before God to love for the rest of your life?

How many times has your love proven incapable of controlling your anger? How many times has your love motivated you to forgive or brought about a peaceable end to an ongoing argument?

It's this failure that exposes mankind's sinful condition. We've all fallen short of God's commands (Romans 3:23). We've all demonstrated selfishness, hatred, and pride. And unless something is done to cleanse us of these ungodly attributes, we will stand before God guilty as charged (Romans 6:23). That's why if you're not right with

God, you can't truly love your spouse because He is the Source of that love.

You can't give what you don't have. You can't call up inner reserves and resources that aren't there to be summoned. In the same way that you can't give away a million dollars if you don't have it to start with, you cannot pay out love in greater measure than you own. You can try, but you will fail.

So the hard news is this: love that is able to withstand every pressure is out of your reach, as long as you're only looking within yourself to find it. You need someone who can give you that kind of love.

"Love is from God" (1 John 4:7). And only those who have allowed Him into their heart through faith in His Son, Jesus — only those who have received the Spirit of Christ through belief in His death and resurrection — are able to tap into love's real power. "Apart from me," Jesus said, "you can do nothing" (John 15:5).

But He also said, "If you abide in Me, and My words abide in you, ask whatever you wish, and it will be done for you" (John 15:7). God has promised through Christ to dwell in your heart through faith so that you can "know the love of Christ which passes knowledge; that you may be filled with all the fullness of God" (Ephesians

3:19 NKJV).

When you surrender yourself to Christ, His power can work through you. Even at your very best, you are not able to live up to God's standards. But He "is able to do far more abundantly beyond all that we ask or think, according to the power that works within us" (Ephesians 3:20). That's how you love your spouse.

So this unsettling secret — as defeating as it may feel — has a happy ending for those who will stop resisting and will receive the love God has for them. This means that the love He has "poured out within our hearts through the Holy Spirit who was given to us" (Romans 5:5) is always available, every time we choose to submit to it.

You simply won't be able to do it without Him.

Perhaps you've never given your heart to Christ, but you sense Him drawing you today. You may be realizing for the first time that you, too, have broken God's commands, and that your guilt will keep you from knowing Him. But Scripture says that if you repent by turning away from your sin and turning to God, He is willing to forgive you because of the sacrifice His Son made on the cross. He is pursuing you, not to enslave you but to free you, so you can receive His love and forgiveness. Then you can share it with the one you've been called most specifically to love.

Perhaps you're already a believer, but you would admit that you have walked away from fellowship with God. You're not in the Word, you're not in prayer, maybe you're not even in church anymore. The love you used to feel coursing through your veins has dwindled into apathy.

The truth is, you can't live without Him and you can't love without Him. But there is no telling what He could do in your marriage if you put your trust in Him.

## TODAY'S DARE

LOOK BACK OVER THE DARES FROM PREVIOUS DAYS. WERE THERE SOME THAT SEEMED IMPOSSIBLE TO YOU? HAVE YOU REALIZED YOUR NEED FOR GOD TO CHANGE YOUR HEART AND TO GIVE YOU THE ABILITY TO LOVE? ASK HIM TO SHOW YOU WHERE YOU STAND WITH HIM, AND ASK FOR THE STRENGTH AND GRACE TO SETTLE YOUR ETERNAL DESTINATION.

___ Check here when you've completed today's dare.

What do you believe God is saying to you? Is there a stirring in your heart? What decision have you made in response to this?

_____

_____

_____

_____

_____

Your receipt
MidPointe Library System
West Chester
513-777-3131
www.MidPointeLibrary.org

**Customer Name:**
 **Trujillo, Jacqueline Alvarez**

**Items that you checked out**

Title:
 The love dare / Stephen and Alex
 Kendrick ; with Lawrence Kimbrough.
ID: 31815116366513
**Due: Tuesday, March 26, 2019**


Total items: 1
Account balance: $0.00
3/5/2019 6:32 PM
Checked out: 1
Overdue: 0
Hold requests: 0
Ready for pickup: 0

Stream free TV shows, movies,
audiobooks and music with hoopla! Visit
hoopladigital.com today!

**Customer Name:**
**Trujillo, Jacqueline Alvarez**

**Items that you checked out**

Title
The love dare / Stephen and Alex
Kendrick ; with Lawrence Kimbrough
ID: 31845145665 13
**Due: Tuesday, March 26, 2019**

Total items: 1
Account balance: $0.00
3/5/2019 6:32 PM
Checked out: 1
Overdue: 0
Hold requests: 0
Ready for pickup: 0

_____

_____

_____

_____

_____

_____

_____

_____

_____

_____

_____

_____

*This is impossible, but with God all things are possible. (Matthew 19:26)*

# DAY 20
## LOVE IS JESUS CHRIST

While we were still helpless, at the right
time Christ died for the ungodly.
— Romans 5:6

The previous day and dare lead to no other
conclusion than this. Thankfully, it's a
conclusion you can live with — today,
tomorrow, and forever.

Jesus has come "to seek and to save" you
(Luke 19:10). Everything you've failed at
and haven't been able to do, every minute
you've wasted trying to fix things your own
way — all of it can be forgiven and made
right by putting your life into the hands of
the One who first gave it to you.

*Maybe you've never done this.* Then today
is your day. "Now is the acceptable time,
behold, now is the day of salvation" (2
Corinthians 6:2).

*Maybe you did it years ago,* but you've
wandered far from your spiritual roots.

Then "repent and return, so that your sins may be wiped away, in order that times of refreshing may come from the presence of the Lord" (Acts 3:19). Even if you've already made Christ your way of life and have never stopped walking in fellowship with Him, the following Scriptures will be a grateful reminder of all He's done for you.

The Bible says we are sinful from birth, from the moment we arrive. "Behold, I was brought forth in iniquity, and in sin my mother conceived me" (Psalm 51:5). "All of us have become like one who is unclean, and all our righteous deeds are like a filthy garment" (Isaiah 64:6). It's not as though God sends innocent people to hell.

We deserve it. We simply can't be good enough to live with a pure and holy God.

However, "God has sent His only begotten Son into the world so that we might live through Him" (1 John 4:9). "Although He existed in the form of God, [He] did not regard equality with God a thing to be grasped, but emptied Himself, taking the form of a bond-servant. . . . He humbled Himself by becoming obedient to the point of death, even death on a cross" (Philippians 2:6–8). "He Himself bore our sins in His body on the cross, so that we might die to sin and live to righteousness; for by His wounds you were healed" (1 Peter 2:24). By His death, He made invalid the very idea that you are unloved and devalued. If you ever feel that way, you're not looking at the cross. He proved His love for you there.

*Love like this cannot be fully understood.* "One will hardly die for a righteous man; though perhaps for the good man someone would dare even to die. But God demonstrates His own love toward us, in that while we were yet sinners, Christ died for us" (Romans 5:7–8).

*Nor can love like this be earned.* "The wages of sin is death, but the free gift of God is eternal life in Christ Jesus our Lord" (Romans 6:23). "For by grace you have been saved through faith; and that not of yourselves, it is the gift of God; not as a result of works, so that no one may boast" (Ephesians 2:8–9).

*But it must be received.* "If you confess with your mouth Jesus as Lord, and believe in your heart that God raised Him from the dead, you will be saved; for with the heart a person believes, resulting in righteousness, and with the mouth he confesses, resulting in salvation" (Romans 10:9–10).

And when you have received this new life and love as your own, you are free to love in ways you've never been capable before.

"This is how we know what love is: Jesus Christ laid down his life for us. And we ought to lay down our lives for our brothers. . . . This is his command: to believe in the name of his Son, Jesus Christ, and to love one another as he commanded us" (1 John 3:16, 23 NIV). "The one who does not love does not know God, for God is love" (1 John 4:8).

He was willing to love you even though you didn't deserve it, even when you didn't love back. He was able to see all your flaws and imperfections and still choose to love you. His love made the greatest sacrifice to meet your greatest need. As a result, you are able (by His grace) to walk in the fullness and blessing of His love. Now and forever.

This means you now share this same love with your spouse. You can love even when you're not loved in return. You can see all their flaws and imperfections and still choose to love. And though you can't meet their needs the way God can, you can become His instrument to meet the needs of your spouse. As result, he or she can walk in the fullness and blessing of your love. Now and till death.

True love is found in Christ alone. And after you have received His gift of new life by accepting His death in your place and His forgiveness for your sins, you are finally ready to live the dare.

## TODAY'S DARE

DARE TO TAKE GOD AT HIS WORD. DARE TO TRUST JESUS CHRIST FOR SALVATION. DARE TO PRAY, "LORD JESUS, I'M A SINNER. BUT YOU HAVE SHOWN YOUR LOVE FOR ME BY DYING TO FORGIVE MY SINS, AND YOU HAVE PROVEN YOUR POWER TO SAVE ME FROM DEATH BY YOUR RESURRECTION. LORD, CHANGE MY HEART, AND SAVE ME BY YOUR GRACE."

__ Check here when you've completed today's dare.

Write about what this experience has been like for you. Even if you are only renewing your commitment to receive and express His love, what has He shown you today?

_____

_____

_____

_____

_____

_____

_____

_____

_____

_____

_____

_____

_____

_____

_____

_____

*In His love and in His mercy He
redeemed them. (Isaiah 63:9)*

# Day 21
## Love is satisfied in God

The Lord will continually guide you, and
satisfy your desire. — Isaiah 58:11

Day 20 was a vitally important day in the
Love Dare — and in your life. You came
face-to-face with the glaring need of every
human heart. And perhaps for the very first
time, you became aware of how personal
this need really is. You may have realized
that nothing in your toolbox of talents and
resources could repair the damage that sin
leaves, and that Jesus is the only One who
can supply what you've been missing. If
you've received Him by faith and have
turned your life over to Him to manage and
lead, then His Holy Spirit is renewing your
heart. His wisdom, grace, and power can
now be released into everything you do.
Including, not the least, your marriage.

But whether this is new territory for you
or if you've been a follower of Jesus for quite

a while, now is the time for you to firm up one thing in your mind: you need God every single day. This is not a part-time proposition. He alone can satisfy, even when all else fails you.

Your husband may be late coming home. Again. But God will always be right on time.

Your wife may let you down. Again. But God can always be trusted to deliver on His promises.

Every day you place expectations on your spouse. Sometimes they meet them. Sometimes they don't. But never will they be able to totally satisfy all the demands you ask of them — partly because some of your demands are unreasonable, partly because your mate is human.

God, however, is not. And those who approach Him in utter dependence each day for the real needs in their life are the ones who find out just how dependable He is.

Can your spouse give you an inner peace? No. But God can. "Be anxious for nothing, but in everything by prayer and supplication with thanksgiving let your requests be made known to God. And the peace of God, which surpasses all comprehension, will guard your hearts and your minds in Christ Jesus" (Philippians 4:6–7).

Can your spouse enable you to be content

no matter what life throws at you? No. But God can. "In any and every circumstance I have learned the secret of being filled. . . . I can do all things through Him who strengthens me" (Philippians 4:12–13).

There are needs in your life only God can fully satisfy. Though your husband or wife is able to complete *some* of these requirements — at least now and then — only God is able to do it all. Your need for love. Your need for acceptance. Your need for joy. It's time to stop expecting somebody or something to keep you functioning and fulfilled on a non-stop basis. Only God can do that as you learn to depend on Him. But He wants to do it His way. "My God will supply all your needs according to His riches in glory in Christ Jesus" (Philippians 4:19).

The needs of love, peace, and adequacy are real. No one is saying you shouldn't have them. But rather than plugging into things that are unstable at best and are subject to change — your health, your money, even the affections and best intentions of your mate — plug into God instead. He's the only One in your life that can *never* change. His faithfulness, His truth, and His promises to His children will always remain. That's why you need to seek Him every day. Our only reason for not doing this is because we really don't trust God to supply what we need. And yet the Bible says, "Delight yourself in the Lord; and He will give you the desires of your heart" (Psalm 37:4). When we are seeking Him first, loving Him first, making our relationship with Him top priority, He promises to supply us with what we really need — which, actually, is all it really takes to satisfy us.

Jesus once spoke to a woman at a Samaritan well, a woman who had tried getting her needs met through a string of failed relationships. With both her life and water bucket empty, she had come to this place broken and hardened yet still desperately in need. But in Christ she found what He called "living water" (John 4:10) — a supply that wasn't just for quenching temporary thirst. What He offered her was a drink of soul satisfaction that never quits giving and refreshing. And that is what's available to you each morning at sunrise and each night before bed, no matter who your spouse is or what they've done to you.

God is your everyday supply. Of everything you need.

## TODAY'S DARE

BE INTENTIONAL TODAY ABOUT MAKING A TIME TO PRAY AND READ YOUR BIBLE. TRY READING A CHAPTER OUT OF PROVERBS EACH DAY (THERE ARE THIRTY-ONE — A FULL MONTH'S SUPPLY), OR READING A CHAPTER IN THE GOSPELS (MATTHEW, MARK, LUKE, AND JOHN). AS YOU DO, IMMERSE YOURSELF IN THE LOVE AND PROMISES GOD HAS FOR YOU. THIS WILL ADD TO YOUR GROWTH AS YOU WALK WITH HIM.

__ Check here when you've completed today's dare.

How do you think spending time daily with God will change your situation and perspective? How can you make Him a bigger part of your day?

_____

_____

_____

_____

_____

_____

_____

_____

_____

_____

_____

_____

_____

_____

_____

_____

_____

*You open Your hand and satisfy the
desire of every living thing.
(Psalm 145:16)*

171

# Day 22
## Love is faithful

I will betroth you to Me in faithfulness.
Then you will know the Lord.
— Hosea 2:20

As Christians, love is the basis of our whole identity. Our spiritual rebirth came about because "God so loved the world, that He gave His only begotten Son, that whoever believes in Him shall not perish, but have eternal life" (John 3:16).

When asked to clarify what the greatest commandments of all were, Jesus answered, "You shall love the Lord your God with all your heart . . . your soul . . . your strength . . . your mind . . . and your neighbor as yourself" (Luke 10:27).

Our love for each other is supposed to be how people distinguish us as Christ's disciples (John 13:35). It is the root and ground of our existence (Ephesians 3:17), meant to be expressed with passion and fervency (1 Peter 4:8). It is a quality that we are to "abound" in more and more (1 Thessalonians 3:12), always getting better at it, becoming increasingly defined by it.

So if love is what we were created to share, what do you do when your love is rejected? How do you handle it when the one to whom you've pledged your life stops accepting the love you're called to give?

The account of the prophet Hosea is one of the most remarkable in the Bible. Against all logic and propriety, God instructed him to marry a prostitute. He wanted Hosea's marriage to show what Heaven's unconditional love looks like towards us. Hosea's union with Gomer produced three children but, as expected, this woman who had long made her living in immorality was not content to stay faithful to one man. So Hosea was left to deal with a broken heart and the shame of abandonment.

He had loved her, but she had spurned his love. They had grown close, but now she had been disloyal and adulterous, rejecting him for the lust of total strangers.

Time passed, and God spoke to Hosea again. God told him to go and reaffirm his love for this woman who had been repeatedly unfaithful. This time she had reached a new low and had to be bought off the slave block, but Hosea paid the price for her redemption and brought her home. Yes, she had treated his love with contempt. She had dealt treacherously with his heart. But he welcomed her back into his life, expressing an unconditional love.

This is a true story, but it was used as a picture of God's love for us. He showers His favor on us without measure, though in return we often don't pay attention. At times we have acted shamefully and deemed His love an intrusion, as if it's keeping us from what we really want. We have rejected Him in many ways — even after receiving His gift of eternal salvation — and yet He still loves us. He still remains faithful.

Even so, His love doesn't keep Him from calling us to account for our mistreatment of Him. We pay more of a price for our rejection than we often realize. Yet He still chooses to respond with grace and mercy. "In Him we have redemption through His blood, the forgiveness of our trespasses, according to the riches of His grace" (Ephesians 1:7). In Him we have the model of what rejected love does. It stays faithful.

Jesus called us to this kind of love in the passage known as the Sermon on the Mount. He said to "love your enemies, do good to those who hate you, bless those who

curse you, pray for those who mistreat you"
(Luke 6:27–28).

"If you love those who love you, what
credit is that to you? For even sinners love
those who love them. If you do good to
those who do good to you, what credit is
that to you? For even sinners do the same"
(Luke 6:32–33).

"Love your enemies, and do good, and
lend, expecting nothing in return; and your
reward will be great, and you will be sons of
the Most High; for He Himself is kind to
ungrateful and evil men" (Luke 6:35).

From the vantage point of the wedding
altar, you would never have dreamed that
the person you married might later become
to you a kind of "enemy," one you would
need to love as an act of almost total
sacrifice. And yet far too often in marriage,
the relationship does indeed dwindle down
to that level. Even to the point of betrayal
or, sadly, to unfaithfulness.

For many, this is the beginning of the end.
Some respond by rapidly moving toward a
tragic divorce. Others, more protective of
their reputation than even their own happiness, decide to keep the charade going. But
they have no intention of liking it — much
less of loving each other again.

This is not the model, however, for the

follower of Christ. If love is to be like His, it must love even when its overtures are returned unwanted. And for your love to be like that, it must be His love to begin with.

You can give undeserved love to your spouse because God gave undeserved love to you — repeatedly, enduringly. Love is often expressed the most to those who deserve it the least.

Ask Him to fill you with the kind of love only He can provide, then purpose to give it to your mate in a way that reflects your gratefulness to God for loving you. That's the beauty of redeeming love. That's the power of faithfulness.

## TODAY'S DARE

LOVE IS A CHOICE, NOT A FEELING. IT IS AN INITIATED ACTION, NOT A KNEE-JERK REACTION. CHOOSE TODAY TO BE COMMITTED TO LOVE EVEN IF YOUR SPOUSE HAS LOST MOST OF THEIR INTEREST IN RECEIVING IT. SAY TO THEM TODAY IN WORDS SIMILAR TO THESE, "I LOVE YOU. PERIOD. I CHOOSE TO LOVE YOU EVEN IF YOU DON'T LOVE ME IN RETURN."

__ Check here when you've completed today's dare.

Why is this kind of love impossible without the love of Christ beating in your heart? How does His presence within you enable you to love, even when it's primarily one-sided?

_____

_____

_____

_____

_____

_____

_____

_____

_____

_____

_____

_____

_____

_____

_____

_____

_____

*I have chosen the faithful way.*
*(Psalm 119:30)*

# DAY 23
## LOVE ALWAYS
### PROTECTS

[Love] always protects.
— 1 Corinthians 13:7 NIV

Marriage is made up of many things, including joys, sorrows, successes, and failures. But when you think about what you want marriage to be like, the furthest thing from your mind is a battleground. However, there are some battles you should be more than willing to fight. These are battles that pertain to protecting your spouse.

Unfortunately your marriage has enemies out there. They come in different forms and use different strategies, but nonetheless they will conspire to destroy your relationship unless you know how to ward them off.

Some are clever and seem attractive, only to undermine your love and appreciation for one another. Others try to lure your heart away from your spouse by feeding you unhealthy fantasies and unrealistic comparisons. It's a battle you must wage to protect your marriage — when love puts on armor and picks up a sword to defend its own. Your mate and your marriage need your constant protection from things like:

*Harmful influences.* Are you allowing certain habits to poison your home? The Internet and television can be productive and enjoyable additions to your life, but they can also bring in destructive content and drain away precious hours from your family. The same thing goes for work schedules that keep you separated from each other for unhealthy amounts of time.

You can't protect your home when you're rarely there, nor when you're relationally disconnected. You have to fight to keep the balance right.

*Unhealthy relationships.* Not everyone has the material to be a good friend. Not every man you hunt and fish with speaks wisely when it comes to matters of marriage. Not every woman in your lunch group has a good perspective on commitment and priorities. In fact, anyone who undermines your marriage does not deserve to be given the title of "friend." And certainly you must be on guard at all times from allowing opposite-sex relationships at work, the gym, or even the church to draw you emotionally away from the one to whom you've already given your heart.

*Shame.* Everyone deals with some level of inferiority and weakness. And because marriage has a way of exposing it all to you and your mate, you need to protect your wife or husband's vulnerability by never speaking negatively about them in public. Their secrets are your secrets (unless, of course, these involve destructive behaviors that are putting you, your children, or themselves in grave danger). Generally speaking, love hides the fault of others. It covers their shame.

*Parasites.* Watch out for parasites. A parasite is anything that latches onto you or your partner and sucks the life out of your marriage. They're usually in the form of addictions, like gambling, drugs, or pornography. They promise pleasure but grow like a disease and consume more and more of your thoughts, time, and money. They steal away your loyalty and heart from those you love. Marriages rarely survive if parasites are present. If you love your spouse, you must destroy any addiction that has your heart. If you don't, it will destroy you.

The Bible speaks plainly about this protective role, often using the analogy of a shepherd. God warned, "My flock has become a prey . . . food for all the beasts of the field." How so? "For lack of a shepherd." Not because these men were too weak to perform their duties but because they didn't pay attention. Instead of watching to make sure that the sheep weren't being picked off by predators, "the shepherds fed themselves and did not feed My flock" (Ezekiel 34:8). They took extra good care of their own needs and appetites but gave little thought to the safety of those under their supervision.

*Wives* — you have a role as protector in your marriage. You must guard your heart from being led away through novels, magazines, and other forms of entertainment that blur your perception of reality and put unfair expectations on your husband. Instead you must do your part in helping him feel strong, while also avoiding talk-show thinking that can lure your attention away from your family. "The wise woman builds her house, but the foolish tears it down with her own hands" (Proverbs 14:1).

*Men* — you are the head of your home. You are the one responsible before God for guarding the gate and standing your ground against anything that would threaten your wife or marriage. This is no small assignment. It requires a heart of courage and a head for preemptive action. Jesus said, "If the head of the house had known at what time of the night the thief was coming, he would have been on the alert and would not have allowed his house to be broken into" (Matthew 24:43). This role is yours. Take it seriously.

## TODAY'S DARE

REMOVE ANYTHING THAT IS HINDERING YOUR RELATIONSHIP, ANY ADDICTION OR INFLUENCE THAT'S STEALING YOUR AFFECTIONS AND TURNING YOUR HEART AWAY FROM YOUR SPOUSE.

__ Check here when you've completed today's dare.

What did you throw out first? Are there others that need to go as well? What do you hope the removal of these things will do for you, your marriage, and your relationship with God?

_____

_____

_____

_____

_____

_____

_____

_____

_____

_____

_____

_____

_____

_____

_____

_____

_____

_____

_____

*You will be restored if you remove*
*unrighteousness far from your tent.*
*(Job 22:23)*

# DAY 24
## LOVE VS. LUST

The world is passing away, and also its lusts; but the one who does the will of God lives forever. — 1 John 2:17

Adam and Eve were supplied with everything they needed in the garden of Eden. They had fellowship with God and intimacy with one another. But after Eve was deceived by the serpent, she saw the forbidden fruit and set her heart on it. Before long, Adam joined in her wishes, and against God's command both of them ate.

That's the progression. From eyes to heart to action. And then follows shame and regret.

We, too, have been supplied with everything we need for a full, productive, enriching life. "We have brought nothing into the world, so we cannot take anything out of it either" (1 Timothy 6:7). But the Bible goes on to say that, having the basics of food and clothing, we should be "content." And Jesus promised these two things would always be provided to God's children (Matthew 6:25–33).

God's blessings, however, go so far beyond these fundamental needs, we could rightly say that we want for nothing. Yet like Adam and Eve, we still want more. So we set our eyes and hearts on seeking worldly pleasure. We try to meet legitimate needs in illegitimate ways. For many it's seeking sexual fulfillment in another person or in pornographic images designed to *feel* like a real person. We look, stare, and fantasize. We try to be discreet but barely turn our eyes away. And once our eyes are captured by curiosity, our hearts become entangled. Then we act on our lust.

We can also lust after possessions or power or prideful ambition. We see what others have and we want it. Our hearts are deceived into saying, "I could be happy if I only had this." Then we make the decision to go after it.

"But those who want to get rich fall into temptation and a snare and many foolish and harmful desires which plunge men into ruin and destruction" (1 Timothy 6:9).

*Lust* is in opposition to love. It means to set your heart and passions on something forbidden. And for a believer it's the first step out of fellowship with the Lord and with others. That's because every object of your lust — whether it's a young coworker or a film actress, or coveting after a half-million dollar house or a sports car — represents the beginnings of a lie. This person or thing that seems to promise sheer satisfaction is more like a bottomless pit of unmet longings.

Lust always breeds more lust. "What is the source of the wars and the fights among you? Don't they come from the cravings that are at war within you? (James 4:1 HCSB). Lust will make you dissatisfied with your husband or wife. It breeds anger, numbs hearts, and destroys marriages. Rather than fullness, it leads to emptiness.

It's time to expose lust for what it really is — a misguided thirst for satisfaction that only God can fulfill. Lust is like a warning light on the dashboard of your heart, alerting you to the fact that you are not allowing God's love to fill you. When your eyes and heart are on Him, your actions will lead you to lasting joy, not to endless cycles of regret and condemnation.

"His divine power has granted to us everything pertaining to life and godliness, through the true knowledge of Him who called us by His own glory and excellence. For by these He has granted to us His precious and magnificent promises, so that by them you may become partakers of the divine nature, having escaped the corruption that is in the world by lust" (2 Peter 1:3–4).

Are you tired of being lied to by lust? Are you fed up with believing that forbidden pleasures are able to keep you happy and content? Then begin setting your eyes on the Word of God. Let His promises of peace and freedom work their way into your heart. Daily receive the unconditional love He has already proven to you through the cross. Focus on being grateful for everything God has already given you rather than choosing discontentment.

You'll find yourself so full on what He provides, you won't be hungry anymore for the junk food of lust.

And while you're at it, set your eyes and heart on your spouse again. "Let your fountain be blessed, and rejoice in the wife of your youth. . . . Be exhilarated always with her love. For why should you, my son, be exhilarated with an adulteress and embrace the bosom of a foreigner? For the ways of a man are before the eyes of the Lord, and He watches all his paths" (Proverbs 5:18–21).

"Do not love the world nor the things in the world. If anyone loves the world, the love of the Father is not in him" (1 John 2:15). Lust is the best this world has to offer, but love offers you the best life in the world.

## Today's Dare

End it now. Identify every object of lust in your life and remove it. Single out every lie you've swallowed in pursuing forbidden pleasure and reject it. Lust cannot be allowed to live in a back bedroom. It must be killed and destroyed — today — and replaced with the sure promises of God and a heart filled with His perfect love.

__ Check here when you've completed today's dare.

What did you identify as an area of lust? What has this pursuit cost you over time? How has it led you away from the person you want to be? Write about your new commitment to seek Him — and to seek your spouse — rather than seeking after foolish desires.

_____

_____

_____

_____

_____

_____

_____

_____

_____

_____

_____

_____

_____

_____

_____

_____

*Act as free men, and do not use your*
*freedom as a covering for evil.*
*(1 Peter 2:16)*

# DAY 25
## LOVE FORGIVES

What I have forgiven, if I have forgiven
anything, I did it for your sakes in the
presence of Christ. — 2 Corinthians 2:10

This one is tough — perhaps the toughest
dare in the book. But if there is to be any
hope for your marriage, this is a challenge
that must absolutely be taken seriously.
Counselors and ministers who deal with
broken couples on a regular basis will tell
you that this is the most complex problem
of all, a rupture that is often the last to be
repaired. It cannot just be considered and
contemplated but must be deliberately put
into practice. Forgiveness has to happen, or
a successful marriage won't.

Jesus painted a vivid image of forgiveness
in His parable of the ungrateful servant. A
man who owed a sizable sum of money was
surprised when his master heard his appeals
for mercy and totally canceled his debt. But

upon being released from this enormous load, the servant did a most unexpected thing: he went to another man who owed him a much smaller amount and demanded immediate payment. When the master heard of it, things changed dramatically in his arrangement with the slave. "His lord, moved with anger, handed him over to the torturers until he should repay all that was owed him" (Matthew 18:34). A day that had begun with joy and relief ended in grief and hopelessness.

Torture. Prison. When you think of unforgiveness, this is what should come to your mind, for Jesus said, "My heavenly Father will also do the same to you, if each of you does not forgive his brother from your heart" (Matthew 18:35).

Imagine you find yourself in a prison-like setting. As you look around, you see a number of cells visible from where you're standing. You see people from your past incarcerated there — people who wounded you as a child. You see people you once called friends but who wronged you at some point in life. You might see one or both of your parents there, perhaps a brother or sister or some other family member. Even your spouse is locked in nearby, trapped with all the others in this jail of your own making.

This prison, you see, is a room in your own heart. This dark, drafty, depressing chamber exists inside you every day. But not far away, Jesus is standing there, extending to you a key that will release every inmate.

No. You don't want any part of it. These people have hurt you too badly. They knew what they were doing and yet they did it anyway — even your spouse, the one you should have been able to count on most of all. So you resist and turn away. You're unwilling to stay here any longer — seeing Jesus, seeing the key in His hand, knowing what He's asking you to do. It's just too much.

But in trying to escape, you make a startling discovery. There is no way out. You're trapped inside with all the other captives. Your unforgiveness, anger, and bitterness have made a prisoner of you as well. Like the servant in Jesus' story, who was forgiven an impossible debt, you have chosen not to forgive and have been handed over to the jailers and torturers. Your freedom is now dependent on your forgiveness.

Coming to this conclusion usually takes us a while. We see all kinds of dangers and risks involved in forgiving others. For instance, what they did was really wrong, whether they admit it or not. They may not even be sorry about it. They may feel perfectly justified in their actions, even going so far as to blame *you* for it. But forgiveness doesn't absolve anyone of blame. It doesn't clear their record with God. It just clears you of having to worry about how to punish them. When you forgive another person, you're not turning them loose. You're just turning them over to God, who can be counted on to deal with them His way. You're saving yourself the trouble of scripting any more arguments or trying to prevail in this situation. It's not about winning and losing anymore. It's about freedom. It's about letting go.

That's why you often hear people who have genuinely forgiven say, "It felt like a weight being lifted off my shoulders." Yes, that's *exactly* what it is. It's like a breath of fresh air rushing into your heart. The stale dankness of the prison house is flooded with light and coolness. For the first time in a long time, you feel at peace. You feel free.

But how do you do it? You release your anger and the responsibility for judging this person to the Lord. "Never take your own revenge, beloved, but leave room for the wrath of God, for it is written, 'Vengeance

is Mine, I will repay,' says the Lord"
(Romans 12:19).

How do you *know* you've done it? You know it when the thought of their name or the sight of their face — rather than causing your blood to boil — causes you to feel sorry for them instead, to pity them, to genuinely hope they get this turned around.

There's so much more that could be said and so many emotional issues you may need to fight through to get there. But great marriages are not created by people who never hurt each other, only by people who choose to keep "no record of wrongs" (1 Corinthians 13:5).

## TODAY'S DARE

WHATEVER YOU HAVEN'T FORGIVEN IN YOUR MATE, FORGIVE IT TODAY. LET IT GO. JUST AS WE ASK JESUS TO "FORGIVE US OUR DEBTS" EACH DAY, WE MUST ASK HIM TO HELP US "FORGIVE OUR DEBTORS" EACH DAY AS WELL. UNFORGIVENESS HAS BEEN KEEPING YOU AND YOUR SPOUSE IN PRISON TOO LONG. SAY FROM YOUR HEART, "I CHOOSE TO FORGIVE."

__ Check here when you've completed today's dare.

What did you forgive your spouse for today? How long have you been carrying the weight of it? What are the possibilities now that you've released this matter to God?

_____

_____

_____

_____

_____

_____

_____

_____

_____

_____

_____

_____

_____

_____

_____

_____

*Father, forgive them; for they do not know what they are doing. (Luke 23:34)*

# Day 26
## Love is responsible

When you judge another, you condemn
yourself, since you, the judge, do the
same things. — Romans 2:1 HCSB

Today will be hard. But as you seek God's
strength and wisdom, you will be able to
get through it. This day could be a milestone
in your marriage if you allow it to be. So
resolve to focus on what the Lord may be
saying to you, and purpose to follow His
leading.

Today is about *personal responsibility.* It's
something we all agree *others* should have,
but we struggle to maintain it ourselves.
Over the past few decades, there's been a
decline in personal responsibility. More and
more, people seem less likely to acknowledge their own mistakes. We see it in politics.
We see it in business. We see it in celebrity
headlines.

But this is not just a problem with the rich

and famous. To find an example of someone who has an excuse for every action, all we have to do is look in the mirror. We are so quick to justify our motives. So quick to deflect criticism. So quick to find fault — especially with our spouse, who is always the easiest one to blame.

We tend to believe that our views are correct, or at least much more correct than our mate's. And we don't believe that anybody, given our same set of circumstances, would act much differently than we have. As far as we're concerned, we're doing the best we can. And our spouse just ought to be glad we're as good to them as we are.

But love doesn't pass the blame so easily or justify selfish motives. Love is not nearly as concerned with its own performance as with others' needs. When love takes responsibility for its actions, it's not to prove how noble you've been but rather to admit how much further you have to go.

Love doesn't make excuses. Love keeps working to make a difference — in you and in your marriage.

That's why the next time you're in an argument with your spouse, instead of working up your comebacks, stop and see if there's something worth listening to in what your mate is saying. What might happen in your relationship if instead of passing blame, you first admitted your own wrongs? As the Scripture says, "Rebuke is more effective for a wise man than a hundred blows on a fool" (Proverbs 17:10 NKJV).

Love is responsible and is willing to admit and correct its faults and errors up front. Are you taking responsibility for this person you chose for yourself as the love of your life? How deliberate are you about making sure your spouse's needs are met? Or are you only concerned with your mate fulfilling yours? Love calls us to take responsibility for our partner in marriage. To love them. To honor them. To cherish them.

Are you taking responsibility for your own faults? Have you said or done things to your spouse — or to God — that are wrong? Love desires to have a right relationship with both God *and* your mate. Once that is right, the stage is set for other areas to fall into place.

A real heart of repentance may take a while to grow in you. Pride is very resistant to responsibility, but humility and honesty before God and your spouse is crucial for a healthy relationship.

This doesn't mean you're always wrong and your spouse is always right. This is not a demand that you become a doormat. But if there is something that's not right between you and God, or you and your spouse, then that should be first priority.

"If we say that we have no sin, we are deceiving ourselves and the truth is not in us" (1 John 1:8). However, "if we confess our sins, [God] is faithful and righteous to forgive us our sins and to cleanse us from all unrighteousness" (1 John 1:9). Confess your areas of sin first, then you'll be on better ground to work things out with your spouse.

In order to walk with God and to keep His favor, you must stay clean before Him. That doesn't mean you can never stumble but that you confess it to God and ask for forgiveness when you do.

Can your spouse say that you have wronged or wounded them in any way and never made it right? Part of taking responsibility is admitting when you've failed and asking for forgiveness. It's time to humble yourself, correct your offenses, and repair the damage. It's an act of love. God wants there to be no unresolved issues between the two of you.

The problem is, to do it sincerely you must swallow your pride and seek forgiveness regardless of how your spouse responds. They *should* forgive you, but your responsibility does not lie with their decision. Admitting your mistakes is *your* responsibility. If they have wronged you, leave that for them to deal with at another time.

Ask God to show you where you have failed in your responsibility, then get right with Him first. Once you've done that, you need to get right with your spouse. It may be the most difficult thing you've ever done, but it is crucial to taking the next step in your marriage and with God. If you are sincere, you may be surprised at the grace and strength God gives you when you take this step.

## TODAY'S DARE

TAKE TIME TO PRAY THROUGH YOUR AREAS OF WRONGDOING. ASK FOR GOD'S FORGIVENESS, THEN HUMBLE YOURSELF ENOUGH TO ADMIT THEM TO YOUR SPOUSE. DO IT SINCERELY AND TRUTHFULLY. ASK YOUR SPOUSE FOR FORGIVENESS AS WELL. NO MATTER HOW THEY RESPOND, MAKE SURE YOU COVER YOUR RESPONSIBILITY IN LOVE. EVEN IF THEY RESPOND WITH CRITICISM, ACCEPT IT BY RECEIVING IT AS COUNSEL.

__ Check here when you've completed today's dare.

What does your mate need to see in order to believe that your confession was more than just words?

_____

_____

_____

_____

_____

_____

_____

_____

_____

_____

_____

_____

_____

_____

_____

_____

_____

*Each one must examine his own
work . . . in regard to himself alone.
(Galatians 6:4)*

# DAY 27
## LOVE ENCOURAGES

Guard my soul and deliver me; do not let
me be ashamed, for I take refuge in You.
— Psalm 25:20

Marriage has a way of altering our vision.
We go in expecting our mate to fulfill our
hopes and to make us happy. But this is an
impossible order for our spouse to fill.
Unrealistic expectations breed disappointment. The higher your expectations, the
more likely your spouse will fail you and
cause you frustration.

If a wife expects her husband to always be
on time, clean up after himself, and understand all her needs, she will likely live most
of her married life in constant disappointment. But if she gets realistic and understands that he's human, forgetful, and
sometimes thoughtless, then she will be
more delighted when he *is* responsible, loving, and kind.

Divorce is nearly inevitable when people refuse to allow their spouses to be human. So there needs to be a transition in your thinking. You must choose to live by *encouragement* rather than by *expectations*. The way your spouse has been for the last ten years is likely what he or she will be in the future apart from your loving encouragement and an intervention from God. Love puts the focus on personal responsibility and improving yourself rather than on demanding more from others.

Jesus painted a picture of this when He talked about the person who saw the "speck" in his brother's eye but didn't notice the "log" in his own.

"How can you say to your brother, 'Let me take the speck out of your eye,' and behold, the log is in your own eye? You hypocrite, first take the log out of your own eye, and then you will see clearly to take the speck out of your brother's eye" (Matthew 7:4–5).

Does your spouse feel like they're living with a speck inspector? Are they routinely on edge, fearful of not living up to your expectations? Would they say they spend most days sensing more of your disapproval than your acceptance?

Perhaps you'd respond by saying that the

problem is not with you but with them. If they really do come up short in a lot of areas, why is that your fault? As far as you're concerned, it takes both of you doing everything you can to make marriage work. If your mate doesn't want you to be so critical, they need to realize that the issues you bring up are legitimate. You're not saying you're perfect, by any means, but it does seem like you should be able to say what you think. Right?

The problem with this kind of attitude is that few people are able to respond to criticism with total objectivity. When it seems clear that someone is unhappy with you — whether by direct confrontation or the silent treatment — it's hard not to take their displeasure personally. Especially in marriage.

After all, unlike any other friendship, your relationship with your spouse began with both of you bending over backwards to please the other. When your mate was your boyfriend or girlfriend, they were completely charmed by your personality. You could almost do no wrong. Your life together was so much easier. And though you didn't expect it to stay that way forever, you certainly didn't see them being so sinful and getting so angry with you. You never expected that this man or woman who promised to love you could get to where they didn't even seem to like you.

So when this stark contrast becomes living reality, your natural reaction is to resist it. During the early days of marriage, you may have been more inclined to listen and make subtle changes. But as the years go by, your spouse's disapproval only tends to entrench you. Rather than making you want to correct things, it makes you want to dig in even deeper.

Love is too smart for that. Instead of putting your mate in a position to rebel, love teaches you to give them room to be themselves. Even if you're the goal-oriented type who places high demands on yourself, love calls you not to project your hard-driving ways onto your mate's performance. You must realize that marriage is a relationship to be enjoyed and savored along the way. It's a unique friendship designed by God Himself where two people live together in flawed imperfection but deal with it by encouraging each other, not *discouraging* them.

The Bible says, "Encourage the exhausted, and strengthen the feeble" (Isaiah 35:3). "Encourage one another and build up one another. . . . Encourage the fainthearted,

215

help the weak, be patient with everyone" (1 Thessalonians 5:11, 14).

Don't you want married life to be a place where you can enjoy free expression of who you are, growing within a safe environment that encourages you even when you fail? Your spouse does too — and love gives them that privilege. If your wife or husband has told you on more than one occasion that you make them feel beat down and defeated, you need to take these words to heart. Make a commitment to daily let go of unrealistic expectations and become your spouse's greatest encourager. And the person they're created by God to be will begin to emerge with new confidence and love for you.

## TODAY'S DARE

ELIMINATE THE POISON OF UNREALISTIC
EXPECTATIONS IN YOUR HOME. THINK OF
ONE AREA WHERE YOUR SPOUSE HAS
TOLD YOU YOU'RE EXPECTING TOO
MUCH, AND TELL THEM YOU'RE SORRY
FOR BEING SO HARD ON THEM ABOUT IT.
PROMISE THEM YOU'LL SEEK TO
UNDERSTAND, AND ASSURE THEM OF
YOUR UNCONDITIONAL LOVE.

__ Check here when you've completed
today's dare.

When you place high expectations on your
spouse that they don't feel internally motivated to attain, what does that tell you about
yourself? What are some better ways to deal
with these disconnects?

_____

_____

_____

_____

_____

_____

_____

_____

_____

_____

_____

_____

_____

_____

_____

_____

_____

_____

*Let us consider how to stimulate one
another to love and good deeds.
(Hebrews 10:24)*

219

# Day 28
## Love makes
### SACRIFICES

He laid down His life for us. We should
also lay down our lives for our brothers.
— 1 John 3:16 HCSB

Life can be hard. But what we usually mean
is that *our* life can be hard. We're the first to
feel it when *we're* the ones being mistreated
or inconvenienced. We're quick to sulk when
*we're* the ones who feel deprived or unappreciated. When life is difficult for us, we
notice.

But too often the only way we notice that
life is hard for our mate is when they start
complaining about it. Then instead of
genuinely caring or rushing in to help, we
might think they just have a bad attitude.
The pain and pressure *they're* under don't
register with us the way it does when it's
*our* pain and pressure. When we want to
complain, we expect everyone to understand
and feel sorry for us.

This doesn't happen when love is at work. Love doesn't have to be jarred awake by your mate's obvious signs of distress. Before worries and troubles have begun to bury them, love has already gone into action mode. It sees the weight beginning to pile up and it steps in to help. That's because love wants you to be sensitive to your spouse.

Love makes sacrifices. It keeps you so tuned in to what your spouse needs that you often respond without being asked. And when you don't notice ahead of time and must be told what's happening, love responds to the heart of the problem.

Even when your mate's stress comes out in words of personal accusation, love shows compassion rather than becoming defensive. Love inspires you to say "no" to what you want, in order to say "yes" to what your spouse needs.

That's what Jesus did. "He laid down His life for us" to show us that "we should also lay down our lives" for others. He taught us that the evidence of love is found in seeing a need in others, then doing all we can to satisfy it. "For I was hungry, and you gave Me something to eat; I was thirsty, and you gave Me something to drink; I was a stranger, and you invited Me in; naked, and you clothed Me; I was sick, and you visited Me; I was in prison, and you came to Me" (Matthew 25:35–36).

These are the types of needs you should be looking for in your wife or husband. Instead of sitting around upset that they're not treating you the way you think they should, let love pick you up out of your self-pity and turn your attention to their needs.

*Is he "hungry"* — needing you sexually, even when you don't feel like it?

*Is she "thirsty"* — craving the time and attention you seem able to give to everyone else?

*Does he feel like a "stranger"* — insecure in his work, needing home to be a refuge and sanctuary?

*Is she "naked"* — frightened or ashamed, desperate for the warm covering of your loving affirmation?

*Is he feeling "sick"* — physically tired and needing you to help guard him from interruptions?

*Does she feel in "prison"* — fearful and depressed, needing some safety and intervention?

Love is willing to make sacrifices to see that the needs of your spouse are given your very best effort and focus. When your mate is overwhelmed and under the gun, love calls you to set aside what seems so essential in your own life to help, even if it's merely the gift of a listening ear.

Often all they really need is just to talk this situation out. They need to see in your two attentive eyes that you truly care about what this is costing them, and you're serious about helping them seek answers. They need you to pray with them about what to do, and then keep following up to see how it's going.

The words "How can I help you?" need to stay fresh on your lips.

The solutions may be simple and easy for you to do, or they may be complex and expensive, requiring time, energy, and great effort. Either way, you should do whatever you can to meet the real needs of the one who is a part of who you are. After all, when you help them, you are also helping yourself. That's the beautiful part of sacrificing for your spouse. Jesus did it for us. And He extends the grace to do it for others.

When the New Testament believers began to walk in love, their lives together were marked by sharing and sacrifice. Their heartbeat was to worship the Lord and to serve His people. "All those who had believed were together and had all things in common; and they began selling their property and possessions and were sharing them with all, as anyone might have need" (Acts 2:44–45). As Paul said to one of these churches in a later decade, "I will most gladly spend and be expended for your souls" (2 Corinthians 12:15). Lives that have been raised from death by Jesus' sacrifice should be ready and willing to make daily sacrifices to meet the needs of others.

## TODAY'S DARE

WHAT IS ONE OF THE GREATEST NEEDS IN YOUR SPOUSE'S LIFE RIGHT NOW? IS THERE A NEED YOU COULD LIFT FROM THEIR SHOULDERS TODAY BY A DARING ACT OF SACRIFICE ON YOUR PART? WHETHER THE NEED IS BIG OR SMALL, PURPOSE TO DO WHAT YOU CAN TO MEET THE NEED.

__ Check here when you've completed today's dare.

How much of your mate's stress is caused by your lack of concern or initiative? When you expressed a desire to help, how did they receive it? Are there other needs you could meet?

_____

_____

_____

_____

_____

_____

_____

_____

_____

_____

_____

_____

_____

_____

_____

_____

*Bear one another's burdens, and thereby*
*fulfill the law of Christ. (Galatians 6:2)*

# Day 29
## Love's Motivation

Render service with a good attitude, as to
the Lord and not to men.
— Ephesians 6:7 HCSB

It doesn't take much experience to discover
that your mate will not always motivate your
love. In fact, many times they will *de-
motivate* it. More often than you'd like, it
will seem difficult to find the inspiration to
demonstrate your love. They may not even
receive it when you try to express it. That's
simply the nature of life, even in fairly
healthy marriages.

But although moods and emotions can
create all kinds of moving motivational
targets, one is certain to stay in the same
place, all the time. When God is your reason
for loving, your ability to love is guaranteed.

That's because love comes from Him.

Think of it like this. When you were a
child, your parents certainly established

rules for you to follow. Your bedtime was at a certain hour. Your room had to be kept mostly clean. Your schoolwork needed to be finished before you could go play. If you were like most people, you bent these rules as often as you obeyed them. And if not for the incentive of force and consequences, you might not have obeyed them at all.

But if you met Christ along the way or received any kind of Bible teaching, you probably were exposed to this idea — "Children, be obedient to your parents in all things, for this is well-pleasing to the Lord" (Colossians 3:20). If you took this to heart at all, you knew you didn't merely have your parents to answer to anymore.

This was no longer a battle of wills between you and a flesh-and-blood authority figure. This was now between you and God. Your mom and dad were just the go-betweens.

As it turns out, however, the relationship between parents and children isn't the only thing enhanced by letting God become your driving motivation. Consider the following areas where pleasing Him should become our goal:

*Work.* "Do your work heartily, as for the

Lord rather than for men" (Colossians 3:23).

*Service.* "Obey those who are your masters on earth, not with external service, as those who merely please men, but with sincerity of heart, fearing the Lord" (Colossians 3:22).

*Everything.* Work hard at "whatever you do . . . knowing that from the Lord you will receive the reward of the inheritance. It is the Lord Christ whom you serve" (Colossians 3:23–24).

*Even marriage.* "Wives, be subject to your husbands, as is fitting in the Lord" (Colossians 3:18). "Husbands, love your wives, just as Christ also loved the church and gave Himself up for her" (Ephesians 5:25).

The love that's demanded from you in marriage is not dependent on your mate's sweetness or suitability. The love between a husband and wife should have one chief objective: honoring the Lord with devotion and sincerity. The fact that it blesses our beloved in the process is simply a wonderful, additional benefit.

This change of focus and perspective is crucial for a Christian. Being able to wake up knowing that God is your source and supply — not just of your own needs but also those of your spouse — changes your whole reason for interacting with your mate.

No longer is it this imperfect person who decides how much love you'll show, but rather it's your omni-perfect God who can use even a flawed person like yourself to bestow loving favor on another.

Has your wife become fairly hard to live with lately? Is her slowness at getting over a disagreement wearing on your patience? Can she not just give it a rest? Don't withhold your love just because she thinks differently from you. Love her "as to the Lord."

Is your husband tuning you out, not saying much, apparently brooding over something he's not interested in sharing? Do you feel hurt by his unwillingness to open up? Are you tired of him being so short with you, not even responding to the children the way he needs to? Don't battle back with a double dose of silence and inattention. Love him anyway. "As to the Lord."

Love motivated by mere duty cannot hold out for very long. And love that is only motivated by favorable conditions can never be assured of sufficient oxygen to keep it breathing. Only love that is lifted up as an offering to God — returned to Him in gratitude for all He's done — is able to sustain itself when all other reasons have lost their ability to energize us.

Those who are fine with mediocre marriages can leave their love to chance and hope for the best. But if you are committed to giving your spouse the best love you possibly can, you need to shoot for love's highest motivation. Love that has God as its primary focus is unlimited in the heights it can attain.

## TODAY'S DARE

BEFORE YOU SEE YOUR SPOUSE AGAIN TODAY, PRAY FOR THEM BY NAME AND FOR THEIR NEEDS. WHETHER IT COMES EASY FOR YOU OR NOT, SAY "I LOVE YOU," THEN EXPRESS LOVE TO THEM IN SOME TANGIBLE WAY. GO TO GOD IN PRAYER AGAIN, THANKING HIM FOR GIVING YOU THE PRIVILEGE OF LOVING THIS ONE SPECIAL PERSON — UNCONDITIONALLY, THE WAY HE LOVES BOTH OF YOU.

__ Check here when you've completed today's dare.

How will this change of motivation affect your relationship and reactions? What does this inspire you to do? What does it inspire you to stop doing?

_____

_____

_____

_____

_____

_____

_As for me and my house, we will serve the Lord. (Joshua 24:15)_

# DAY 30
## LOVE BRINGS UNITY

Father, keep them in Your name, the
name which You have given Me, that they
may be one even as We are.
— John 17:11

One of the most impressive things about
the Bible is the way it is linked together,
with consistent themes running throughout,
from beginning to end. Though written over
a span of 1,600 years and composed by
more than forty writers of various backgrounds and skill levels, God sovereignly
authored it with one united voice. And He
continues to speak through it today without
ever going off-message.

Unity. Togetherness. Oneness.

These are the unshakable hallmarks of our
God.

From the very beginning of time, we see
His unity at work through the Trinity —
Father, Son, and Holy Spirit. God the

Father is there, creating the heavens and the earth. The Spirit is "moving over the surface of the waters" (Genesis 1:2). And the Son, who is "the radiance of His glory and the exact representation of His nature" (Hebrews 1:3), joins in speaking the world into existence. "Let Us make man in Our image, according to Our likeness" (Genesis 1:26).

Us. Our.

All three are in perfect oneness of mind and purpose.

We later see Jesus rising from the waters of baptism, as the Spirit descends like a dove and the Father announces over this majestic scene, "This is My beloved Son, in whom I am well-pleased" (Matthew 3:17).

Jesus later says, "I have come down from heaven, not to do My own will, but the will of Him who sent Me" (John 6:38). His desire to answer His followers' prayers is "so that the Father may be glorified in the Son" (John 14:13). He asks the Father to send the Holy Spirit, knowing that the Spirit will faithfully testify about the Son He loves, for "no one knows the thoughts of God except the Spirit of God" (1 Corinthians 2:11 NIV).

Father, Son, and Spirit are in pristine unity. They serve each other, love each other, and honor each other. Though equal, they rejoice when the other is praised. Though distinct, they are one, indivisible.

And because this relationship is so special — so representative of the vastness and grandeur of God — He has chosen to let us experience an aspect of it. In the unique relationship of husband and wife, two distinct individuals are spiritually united into "one flesh" (Genesis 2:24). And "what God has joined together, let man not separate" (Mark 10:9 NIV).

In fact, this mystery is so compelling — and the love between husband and wife so intertwined and complete — that God uses the imagery of marriage to explain His love for the church.

The church (the bride) is most honored when her Savior is worshiped and celebrated. Christ (the bridegroom), who has given Himself up for her, is most honored when He sees her "as a radiant church, without stain or wrinkle or any other blemish, but holy and blameless" (Ephesians 5:27 NIV). Both Christ and the church love and honor the other.

That's the beauty of unity.

*Husband* — What would happen in your marriage if you devoted yourself to loving, honoring, and serving your wife in all things? What if you determined that the preservation of your oneness with this woman was worth every sacrifice and expression of love you could make? What would change in your home if you took that approach to your relationship on a daily basis?

*Wife* — What would happen if you made it your mission to do everything possible to promote togetherness of heart with your husband? What if every threat to your unity was treated as a poison, a cancer, an enemy to be eliminated by love, humility, and selflessness? What would your marriage become if you were never again willing to see your oneness torn apart?

The unity of the Trinity, as seen from beyond the reaches of history past and continuing into the future, is evidence of the power of oneness. It is unbreakable. It is unending. And it is this same spiritual reality that disguises itself as your home and mailing address. Though painted in the colors of work schedules and doctor visits and trips to the grocery, oneness is the eternal thread that runs through the daily experience of what you call "your marriage," giving it a purpose to be defended for life.

Therefore, love this one who is as much a part of your body as you are. Serve this one whose needs cannot be separated from your own. Honor this one who, when raised upon the pedestal of your love, raises you up too in the eyes of God, all at the same time.

## TODAY'S DARE

ISOLATE ONE AREA OF DIVISION IN YOUR
MARRIAGE, AND LOOK ON TODAY AS A
FRESH OPPORTUNITY TO PRAY ABOUT IT.
ASK THE LORD TO REVEAL ANYTHING IN
YOUR OWN HEART THAT IS THREATENING
ONENESS WITH YOUR SPOUSE. PRAY
THAT HE WOULD DO THE SAME
FOR THEM. AND IF APPROPRIATE,
DISCUSS THIS MATTER OPENLY,
SEEKING GOD FOR UNITY.

___ Check here when you've completed
today's dare.

Did the Lord open your eyes to anything
new that might be giving fuel to this point
of disagreement? How do you intend to
respond? What do you hope to see God do
in your spouse as well?

_____

_____

_____

_____

_____

241

_____

_____

_____

_____

_____

_____

_____

_____

_____

_____

_____

_____

*The Lord is our God, the Lord is one!*
*(Deuteronomy 6:4)*

243

# DAY 31
## LOVE AND MARRIAGE

A man shall leave his father and his mother, and be joined to his wife; and they shall become one flesh.
— Genesis 2:24

This verse is God's original blueprint for how marriage is supposed to work. It involves a tearing away and a knitting together. It reconfigures existing relationships while establishing a brand new one. Marriage changes everything.

That's why couples who don't take this "leaving" and "cleaving" message to heart will reap the consequences down the line, when the problems are much harder to repair without hurting someone.

"Leaving" means that you are breaking a natural tie. Your parents step into the role of counselors to be respected, but can no longer tell you what to do. Sometimes the difficulty in doing this comes from the original source. A parent may not be ready to release you yet from their control and expectations. Whether through unhealthy dependence or inner struggles over the empty nest, parents don't always take their share of this responsibility. In such cases, the grown child has to make "leaving" a courageous choice of his own. And far too often, this break is not made in the right way.

Are you and your spouse still living with unresolved issues because of a failure to cut the apron strings? Do either of your parents continue to create problems within your home — perhaps without their even knowing it? What needs to happen to put a stop to this before it creates too wide of a division in your marriage?

Unity is a marriage quality to be guarded at great cost. The purpose of "leaving," of course, is not to abandon all contact with the past but rather to preserve the unique oneness that marriage is designed to capture. Only in oneness can you become all that God means for you to be.

If you're too tightly drawn to your parents, the singular identity of your marriage will not be able to come to flower. You will always be held back, and a root of division will continue to send up new shoots into your relationship. It won't go away unless you do something about it. For without "leaving," you cannot do the "cleaving" you need, the joining of your hearts that's required to experience oneness.

"Cleaving" carries the idea of catching someone by pursuit, clinging to them as your new rock of refuge and safety. This man is now the spiritual leader of your new home, tasked with the responsibility of loving you "just as Christ also loved the church and gave Himself up for her" (Ephesians 5:25). This woman is now one in union with you, called to "see to it that she respects her husband" (Ephesians 5:33).

As a result of this essential process, you are now free to become everything God meant when He declared you "one flesh."

- You are able to achieve oneness in your *decision making,* even when you begin from differing viewpoints.
- You are able to achieve oneness in your *priorities,* even though you've come together from backgrounds that could hardly be more different.
- You are able to achieve oneness in your *sexual affections* toward each other, even if either or both of you have

memories of impurity in your pre-marital past.

God's decision to make you "one flesh" in marriage can make anything possible.

If this is not how things are going in your home right now, you're unfortunately in the majority. It's not out of character for couples of all kinds — even Christian couples — to ignore God's design for marriage, thinking they know better than He does. Genesis 2:24 may have sounded nice and noble when it was wrapped around the sharing of vows at the wedding. But as a fundamental principle to be put into place and practiced as a living fact — this just seems too difficult to do. But this is what you must make any sacrifice to reclaim.

It's hard — extremely hard — when the pursuit of oneness is basically one-sided. Your spouse may not be interested at all in recapturing the unity you had at first. Even if there *is* some desire on his or her part, there may still be issues between you that are nowhere close to being resolved.

But if you'll continue to keep a passion for oneness forefront in your mind and heart, your relationship over time will begin to reflect the inescapable "one flesh" design that is printed on its DNA. You don't have to go looking for it. It's already there. But you do have to live it, or there's nothing else to expect than disunity.

Leave. And cleave. And dare to walk as one.

## TODAY'S DARE

IS THERE A "LEAVING" ISSUE YOU
HAVEN'T BEEN BRAVE ENOUGH TO
CONQUER YET? CONFESS IT TO YOUR
SPOUSE TODAY, AND RESOLVE TO MAKE
IT RIGHT. THE ONENESS OF YOUR
MARRIAGE IS DEPENDENT UPON IT.
FOLLOW THIS WITH A COMMITMENT TO
YOUR SPOUSE AND TO GOD TO MAKE
YOUR MARRIAGE THE TOP PRIORITY OVER
EVERY OTHER HUMAN RELATIONSHIP.

__ Check here when you've completed
today's dare.

Has this been a hard thing for you to deal
with? How has it affected your relationship?
If the worse offender in this area is your
spouse (with your in-laws), how can you
lovingly move this toward a better situation?

_____

_____

_____

_____

_____

_____

_____

_____

_____

_____

_____

_____

_____

_____

_____

_____

*May they all be one, as You, Father, are in Me and I am in You. (John 17:21 HCSB)*

# Day 32
## Love meets sexual needs

The husband must fulfill his duty to his wife, and likewise also the wife to her husband. — 1 Corinthians 7:3

Some people think the Bible has nothing good to say about sex, as though all God seems concerned about is telling us when not to do it and who not to do it with. In reality, however, the Bible has a great deal to say about sex and the blessing it can be for both husband and wife. Even its boundaries and restrictions are God's ways of keeping our sexual experiences at a level far beyond any of those advertised on television or in the movies.

In Christian marriage, romance is meant to thrive and flourish. After all, it was created by God. It's all part of celebrating what God has given, becoming one with our mate while simultaneously pursuing purity and holiness. He delights in us when this happens.

The Song of Solomon, for example, though frequently misunderstood as nothing more than an allegory about God's passion for His people, is actually a beautiful love story. It describes sexual acts between a husband and wife in poetic detail, showing how each one responds to the other. It expresses how honesty and understanding in sexual matters lead to a life of confident love together.

It's true that sex is only one aspect of marriage. But as time goes by, one of you will likely value its importance more highly than the other. As a result of this, the nature of your oneness as man and wife will feel threatened and endangered.

Again, the biblical foundations of marriage were originally expressed in the creation of Adam and Eve. She was made to be "a helper suitable for him" (Genesis 2:18). The unity of their relationship and physical bodies was so strong, they were said to become "one flesh" (Genesis 2:24).

This same oneness is a hallmark of every marriage. In the act of romance, we join our hearts to each other in an expression of love that no other form of communication can match. That's why "the marriage bed is to be undefiled" (Hebrews 13:4). We are not to share this same experience with anyone else.

But we are weak. And when this legitimate need goes unmet — when it's treated as being selfish and demanding by the other — our hearts are subject to being drawn away from marriage, tempted to fulfill this longing somewhere else, some other way.

To counteract this tendency, God established marriage with a "one flesh" mentality. "The wife does not have authority over her own body, but the husband does; and likewise also the husband does not have authority over his own body, but the wife does" (1 Corinthians 7:4).

Sex is not to be used as a bargaining chip. It is not something God allows us to withhold without consequence. Though there can certainly be abuses to this divinely designed framework, the heart of marriage is one of giving ourselves to each other to meet the other's needs.

Sex is one God-given opportunity to do that.

So "stop depriving one another," the Bible warns, "except by agreement for a time, so that you may devote yourselves to prayer, and come together again so that Satan will not tempt you because of your lack of self-control" (1 Corinthians 7:5).

You are the one person called and designated by God to meet your spouse's sexual needs. If you allow distance to grow between you in this area, if you allow staleness to set in, you are taking something that rightly (and exclusively) belongs to your spouse. If you let your mate know — by words, actions, or inactions — that sex needn't be any more than you want it to be, you rob from them a sense of honor and endearment that has been set in place by biblical mandate. You violate the "one flesh" unity of marriage.

So whether you perceive yourself as being on the deprived end, or you would admit that you are the one depriving the other, know that God's plan for you is to meet in the middle and come to a place of agreement. But also know that the path to getting there will not be accomplished by sulking, arguing, or demanding. Love is the only way to reestablish loving union between each other. All the things the Love Dare entails — patience, kindness, selflessness, thoughtfulness, protection, honor, forgiveness — will play a role in renewing your sexual intimacy. When the love of Christ is the foundation of your marriage, the strength of your friendship and sexual relationship can be enjoyed at a level this world can never know.

"You have been bought with a price," God has declared (1 Corinthians 6:20). He set His affections on you and went to every length to draw you into desiring Him. Now it is your turn to pay the loving price to win the heart of your mate. When you do, you will enjoy the pure delight that flows when sex is done for all the right reasons. And as if that's not enough, you will also have the opportunity to "glorify God in your body" (1 Corinthians 6:20). How beautiful.

## TODAY'S DARE

IF AT ALL POSSIBLE, TRY TO INITIATE SEX WITH YOUR HUSBAND OR WIFE TODAY. DO THIS IN A WAY THAT HONORS WHAT YOUR SPOUSE HAS TOLD YOU (OR IMPLIED TO YOU) ABOUT WHAT THEY NEED FROM YOU SEXUALLY. ASK GOD TO MAKE THIS ENJOYABLE FOR BOTH OF YOU AS WELL AS A PATH TO GREATER INTIMACY.

__ Check here when you've completed today's dare.

Was this a satisfying experience for you? If it didn't turn out the way you'd hoped, what do you think is complicating matters? Have you committed this to prayer? If it was a true blessing for both of you, what can you learn from this for the future?

_____

_____

_____

_____

_____

_How beautiful and how delightful you are,
my love. (Song of Solomon 7:6)_

# DAY 33
## LOVE COMPLETES
### EACH OTHER

If two lie down together they keep warm,
but how can one be warm alone?
— Ecclesiastes 4:11

God creates marriage by taking a man and a woman and uniting them as one. And although love must be willing to act alone if necessary, it is always better when it is not just a solo performance. Love can function on its own if there is no other way, but there is a "more excellent way" (1 Corinthians 12:31). And love dares not to stop loving before it gets there.

This "completing" aspect of love was revealed to mankind from the beginning. God originated the human race with a male and a female — two similar but complementary designs meant to function in harmony.

Our bodies are made for each other. Our natures and temperaments provide balance, enabling us to more effectively complete the tasks at hand. Our oneness can produce children, and our teamwork can best raise them to health and maturity. Where one is weak, the other is strong. When one needs building up, the other is equipped to enhance and encourage. We multiply one another's joys and divide one another's sorrows.

The Scriptures say, "Two are better than one because they have a good return for their labor. For if either of them falls, the one will lift up his companion. But woe to the one who falls when there is not another to lift him up" (Ecclesiastes 4:9, 10). It's like your two hands, which don't just coexist together but multiply the effectiveness of the other. In order to do what they do, neither is quite complete without the other.

Although our differences can frequently be the source of misunderstanding and conflict, they have been created by God and can be ongoing blessings if we respect them.

One of you may be better at cooking, for instance, while the other is more thorough in cleaning the dishes. One may be more gentle and able to keep peace among family members, while the other handles discipline more directly and effectively. One may have a good business head but needs the other to help him remember to be generous.

When we learn to accept these distinctions in our mate, we can bypass criticism and go straight to helping and appreciating one another.

But some can't seem to get past their partner's differences. And they suffer many wasted opportunities as a result. They don't take advantage of the uniqueness that makes each of them more effective when including the other.

One such example from the Bible is Pontius Pilate, the Roman governor who presided over the trial of Jesus. Unaware of who Christ was and against his better judgment, he allowed the crowd to influence him into crucifying Jesus.

But the one person who was more sensitive to what was really happening was Pilate's wife, who came to him at the height of the uproar and warned him he was making a mistake. "While he was sitting on the judgment seat, his wife sent him a message, saying, 'Have nothing to do with that righteous Man; for last night I suffered greatly in a dream because of Him' " (Matthew 27:19).

She was apparently a woman of keen discernment who grasped the magnitude of these events before her husband did. Certainly, God's sovereignty was at work, and nothing would have kept His Son from marching obediently to the cross for us. But Pilate's dismissal of his wife's intuition reveals an unfortunate side to man's nature that is often downplayed. God made wives to complete their husbands, and He gives them insight that in many cases is kept from their men. If this discernment is ignored, it is often to the detriment of the man making the decision.

The effectiveness of your marriage is dependent upon both of you working together. Do you have big decisions to make about your finances or retirement planning? Are you having a real problem with a coworker who's getting harder and harder to deal with, and you are grappling with the appropriate action to take? Are you absolutely convinced that your educational choices for the children are right, no matter what your spouse thinks?

Don't try doing all the analysis yourself. Don't disqualify his or her right to voice an opinion on matters that affect both of you. Love realizes that God has put you together on purpose. And though you may wind up disagreeing with your spouse's perspectives, you should still give their views respect and strong consideration. This honors God's design for your relationship and guards the oneness He intends.

Joined together, you are greater than your independent parts. You need each other. You complete each other.

## TODAY'S DARE

RECOGNIZE THAT YOUR SPOUSE IS INTEGRAL TO YOUR FUTURE SUCCESS. LET THEM KNOW TODAY THAT YOU DESIRE TO INCLUDE THEM IN YOUR UPCOMING DECISIONS, AND THAT YOU NEED THEIR PERSPECTIVE AND COUNSEL. IF YOU HAVE IGNORED THEIR INPUT IN THE PAST, ADMIT YOUR OVERSIGHT AND ASK THEM TO FORGIVE YOU.

__ Check here when you've completed today's dare.

What are some upcoming decisions you can make together? What did you learn today about the role of your mate?

_____

_____

_____

_____

_____

_____

_Put on love, which is the perfect bond of_
_unity. (Colossians 3:14)_

# DAY 34
## LOVE CELEBRATES
### GODLINESS

[Love] does not rejoice in
unrighteousness, but rejoices with the
truth. — 1 Corinthians 13:6

From the moment you close your Bible in
the morning, nearly everything else you'll
encounter throughout the day will be luring
you away from its truths. The opinions of
your coworkers, the news coverage on
television, your typical Web sites, the various temptations of the day — all of these
and more will be working overtime to shape
your perceptions of what's true and most
desirable in life.

They'll say that having a knockout wife
who dresses to get other men's attention is
a good thing. They'll say that bad language
and immorality in the movies are fine for
mature people. They'll say that church isn't
important in a person's life. They'll say that
we each must find God in our own way.

They'll say a lot of things. And they'll say them so loudly and frequently that if we're not careful, we can start believing that what they say is the way things should be. We can begin valuing what everybody else values and thinking the way everybody else does.

But the meaning of "real life" changes dramatically when we understand that God's Word is the ultimate expression of what real life is. The teachings it contains are not just good guesses at what should matter. They are principles that reflect the way things really are, the way God created life to be. His ideals and instructions are the only pathways to real blessing, and when we see people following them in obedience to the Lord, it should cause us to rejoice.

What makes you the proudest of your husband? Is it when he comes home with a trophy from the company golf tournament, or when he gathers the family before bedtime to pray together and read the Word?

What overjoys you the most in your wife? Is it seeing her try a new painting technique in the children's bedrooms, or seeing her forgive the neighbor whose dog dug up her plants?

You are one of the most influential people in your spouse's life. Have you been using your influence to lead them to honor God, or to dishonor Him?

Love rejoices most in the things that please God. When your mate is growing in Christian character, persevering in faith, seeking purity, and embracing roles of giving and service — becoming spiritually responsible in your home — the Bible says we should be celebrating it. The word "rejoices" in 1 Corinthians 13:6 carries the idea of being absolutely thrilled, excitedly cheering them on for what they're allowing God to accomplish in their lives.

The apostle Paul, who helped establish and minister to many of the first-century churches, wrote in his letters how delighted he was to hear reports of the people's faithfulness and growth in Jesus. "We ought always to give thanks to God for you, brethren, as is only fitting, because your faith is greatly enlarged, and the love of each one of you toward one another grows ever greater; therefore, we ourselves speak proudly of you among the churches of God for your perseverance and faith in the midst of all your persecutions and afflictions which you endure" (2 Thessalonians 1:3–4).

The apostle John, who had walked closely with Jesus and became one of the main leaders in the early church, once wrote to his flock, "I have no greater joy than this, to hear of my children walking in the truth" (3 John 4).

That should be what energizes us when we see it happening in our mate. More than when they save money on the grocery bill. More than when they achieve success at work. Sometimes by accepting modern culture's take on what to applaud in our spouse, we can even be guilty of encouraging them to sin — perhaps by feeding their vanity, or by letting boys be boys.

But "love does not rejoice in unrighteousness" — not in ourselves and not in our mate. Rather, love "rejoices with the truth," the way Paul did when he said to the Roman church, "The report of your obedience has reached to all; therefore I am rejoicing over you, but I want you to be wise in what is good and innocent in what is evil" (Romans 16:19). He knew that the pursuit of godliness, purity, and faithfulness was the only way for them to find joy and ultimate fulfillment. Being "wise" about holiness while being "innocent" about sin — remaining unjaded and uncompromising as we travel through life — is the way to win in God's eyes.

And what more could we want for our wife or husband than for them to experience God's best in life?

Be happy for any success your spouse enjoys. But save your heartiest congratulations for those times when they are honoring God with their worship and obedience.

## TODAY'S DARE

FIND A SPECIFIC, RECENT EXAMPLE WHEN YOUR SPOUSE DEMONSTRATED CHRISTIAN CHARACTER IN A NOTICEABLE WAY. VERBALLY COMMEND THEM FOR THIS AT SOME POINT TODAY.

__ Check here when you've completed today's dare.

What example did you choose to recognize? How many other ways could you celebrate their growth in godliness? How could you encourage them to persevere in it?

_____

_____

_____

_____

_____

_____

_____

_____

_____

_____

_____

_____

_____

_____

_____

_____

_____

_____

*I will walk within my house in the integrity
of my heart. (Psalm 101:2)*

# DAY 35
## LOVE IS ACCOUNTABLE

Plans fail for lack of counsel, but with
many advisers they succeed.
— Proverbs 15:22 NIV

Mighty sequoia trees tower hundreds of feet
in the air and can withstand intense environ-
mental pressures. Lightning can strike them,
fierce winds can blow, and forest fires can
rage around them. But the sequoia endures,
standing firm, only growing stronger
through the trials.

One of the secrets to the strength of this
giant tree is what goes on below the surface.
Unlike many trees, they reach out and
interlock their roots with the sequoias
around them. Each becomes empowered
and reinforced by the strength of the others.

The secret to the sequoia is also a key to
maintaining a strong, healthy marriage. A
couple that faces problems alone is more

likely to fall apart during tough times. However, the ones who interlock their lives in a network of other strong marriages radically increase their chances of surviving the fiercest of storms. It is crucial that a husband and wife pursue godly advice, healthy friendships, and experienced mentors.

Everyone needs wise counsel throughout life. Wise people constantly seek it and gladly receive it. Fools never ask for it and then ignore it when it's given to them.

As the Bible so clearly explains, "The way of a fool is right in his own eyes, but a wise man is he who listens to counsel" (Proverbs 12:15).

Gaining wise counsel is like having a detailed road map and a personal guide while traveling on a long, challenging journey. It can be the difference between continual success or the destruction of another marriage. It is vital that you invite strong couples to share the wisdom they have gained through their own successes and failures.

Why waste years of your life learning painful lessons when you could discover those same truths during a few hours of wise counsel? Why not cross the bridges others have built? Wisdom is more valuable than gold. Not receiving it is like letting priceless coins pass through your fingers.

Good marriage mentors warn you before you make a bad decision. They encourage you when you are ready to give up. And they cheer you on as you reach new levels of intimacy in your marriage.

Do you have an older couple or a friend of the same gender you can turn to for good advice, for prayer support, and for regular accountability check-ups? Do you have someone in your life who shoots straight with you?

You and your spouse need these types of friends and mentors on a consistent basis. The Bible says, "Encourage one another day after day . . . so that none of you will be hardened by the deceitfulness of sin" (Hebrews 3:13). Too often we can isolate ourselves from others. If we are not careful, we could push away the people who love us the most.

You must guard yourself against the wrong influencers. Everyone has an opinion and some people will encourage you to act selfishly and leave your mate in order to pursue your own happiness. Be careful about listening to advice from people who don't have a good marriage themselves.

If your marriage is hanging by a thread or already heading for a divorce, then you need to stop everything and pursue solid counseling as quickly as possible. Call a pastor, a Bible-believing counselor, or a marriage ministry today. As awkward as it may initially be to open up your life to a stranger, your marriage is worth every second spent and every sacrifice you will make for it. Even if your marriage is fairly stable, you're in no less need of honest, open mentors — people who can put wind in your sails and make your marriage even better.

How do you pick a good mentor? You look for a person who has the kind of marriage you want. You look for a person whose heart for Christ comes first before everything else. You look for someone who doesn't live by his or her opinions but by the unchanging Word of God. And more times than not, this person will likely be delighted you asked for help. Start praying for God to send this person into your life. Then pick a time to meet and talk.

If this doesn't sound too important to you, it would be a good idea to ask yourself why. Do you have something to hide? Are you afraid you will be embarrassed? Do you think your marriage is exempt from needing outside help? Does diving into a river of positive influence not appeal to you? Don't be the captain of another Titanic divorce by ignoring the warning signs around you when you could have been helped.

Here's an important reminder from Scripture: "Each one of us will give an account of himself to God" (Romans 14:12). This appointment is unbreakable. And though we're all ultimately responsible for the way we approach it, we can surely stand as much help as others can give. It might just be the relational influence that takes your marriage from mediocre to amazing.

## TODAY'S DARE

FIND A MARRIAGE MENTOR — SOMEONE WHO IS A STRONG CHRISTIAN AND WHO WILL BE HONEST AND LOVING WITH YOU. IF YOU FEEL THAT COUNSELING IS NEEDED, THEN TAKE THE FIRST STEP TO SET UP AN APPOINTMENT. DURING THIS PROCESS, ASK GOD TO DIRECT YOUR DECISIONS AND DISCERNMENT.

__ Check here when you've completed today's dare.

Who did you choose? Why did you select this person? What do you hope to learn from them?

_____

_____

_____

_____

_____

_____

_In abundance of counselors there is victory. (Proverbs 11:14)_

# DAY 36
## LOVE IS GOD'S WORD

*Your word is a lamp to my feet and a light to my path.* — Psalm 119:105

For some people, the Bible seems just too big to understand. It's like an impossible challenge. They don't know where or how to begin. But as a Christian, you're not left alone to try grasping the major themes and deep meanings of the Bible. The Holy Spirit, who now lives in your heart by way of salvation, is an illuminator of truth. "For the Spirit searches all things, even the depths of God" (1 Corinthians 2:10). And because of His internal lamp, the Scriptures are now yours to read, absorb, comprehend, and live by.

But first, you've got to commit to do it.

*Be in it.* If this is not already a habit of yours, now is the time to begin reading a portion of the Bible every day. Ideally, read it together as husband and wife — in the morning, perhaps, or before bed. Be like the writer of Psalm 119, who could say, "With all my heart I have sought You. . . . Your word I have treasured in my heart, that I may not sin against You" (Psalm 119:10–11).

Those who practice a consistent pattern of reading the Bible soon discover it to be "more desirable than gold, yes, than much fine gold; sweeter also than honey and the drippings of the honeycomb" (Psalm 19:10).

*Stay under it.* You're right, the Bible can be deep and challenging. That's why it's so important to be part of a church where the Word is faithfully taught and preached. By hearing it explained in sermons and Bible study classes, you'll get a broader, more balanced view of what God is saying through His Word. You'll also get to join with others who are on the same journey you are, wanting to be fed by the truths of Scripture. "Continue in the things you have learned and become convinced of, knowing from whom you have learned them" (2 Timothy 3:14).

*Live it.* Unlike most other books, which are

only designed to be read and digested, the Bible is a *living* book. It lives because the Holy Spirit still resonates within its words. It lives because, unlike the ancient writings of other religions, its Author is still alive. And it lives because it becomes a part of who you are, how you think, and what you do. "Prove yourselves doers of the word, and not merely hearers" (James 1:22).

Jesus talked about people who build their lives on sand — their own logic, their best guesses, the latest reasoning. When the storms of life begin to blow (which they always will), foundations of sand will only result in total disaster. Their houses may light up and look nice for a while, but they are tragedies waiting to happen. Ultimately they collapse.

But Jesus said, "Everyone who hears these words of Mine and acts on them, may be compared to a wise man who built his house on the rock. The rain fell, and the floods came, and the winds blew and slammed against that house; and yet it did not fall, for it had been founded on the rock" (Matthew 7:24–25). When your home is founded on the rock of God's unchanging Word, it is insured against destruction.

That's because God has the right plan for everything, and He's revealed these plans in

His Word. They're right there for anyone who will read it and apply it.

God has a plan for the way you handle your money. A plan for the way you raise your children. A plan for the way you treat your body. A plan for the way you spend your time. A plan for the way you handle conflict. Isn't it just like your Maker to know exactly what you need?

If being a regular Bible reader is new for you, you'll be surprised how quickly you'll begin thinking differently and more eternally. And if you are serious about establishing strategies for life based on God's way of doing things, He will guide you to make connections between what you're reading and how it applies. It's an enlightening journey with discoveries to be made all the time.

Every aspect of your life that you submit to, God's principles will grow stronger and more long-lasting over time. But any part you withhold from Him, choosing instead to try your own hand at it, will weaken and eventually fail when the storms of life hit you. It may, in fact, be the one area that hastens the downfall of your home and marriage.

Wise couples build their houses on the rock of God's Word. They've seen what sand can do. They know how it feels when their footing gets soft and the foundation gives way. That's why you must determine to build your life and marriage on the solid rock of the Bible, and then you can plan on a stronger future — no matter how bad the storms get.

## TODAY'S DARE

COMMIT TO READING THE BIBLE EVERY DAY. FIND A DEVOTIONAL BOOK OR OTHER RESOURCE THAT WILL GIVE YOU SOME GUIDANCE. IF YOUR SPOUSE IS OPEN TO IT, SEE IF THEY WILL COMMIT TO DAILY BIBLE READING WITH YOU. BEGIN SUBMITTING EACH AREA OF YOUR LIFE TO ITS GUIDANCE AND START BUILDING ON THE ROCK.

__ Check here when you've completed today's dare.

What parts of your life are in the greatest need of God's counsel? Where do you feel the most susceptible to failure? What are you asking God to show you through His Word?

_____

_____

_____

_____

_____

_____

_____

_____

_____

_____

_____

_____

_____

_____

_____

*For a way to familiarize yourself with the
Bible, see Appendix III*

*Whatever was written in earlier times was
written for our instruction. (Romans 15:4)*

# Day 37

## Love Agrees in

### Prayer

If two of you agree on earth about anything
that they may ask, it shall be done for
them by My Father. — Matthew 18:19

If someone told you that by changing one
thing about your marriage, you could guarantee with near 100 percent assurance that
your life together would significantly improve, you would at least want to know what
it was. And for many godly couples, that
"one thing" is the daily practice of praying
together.

To someone who tends to devalue spiritual
matters, this sounds fairly ridiculous. And if
told that shared prayer is a key ingredient in
marital longevity and leads to a heightened
sense of sexual intimacy, they would think
you had really gone too far. But the unity
that grows between a man and woman who
regularly pray together forms an intense and
powerful connection. Within the sanctuary

of your marriage, praying together can work wonders on every level of your relationship.

When you were joined together as husband and wife, God gave you a wedding gift — a permanent prayer partner for life. When you need wisdom on a certain decision, you and your prayer partner can seek God together for the answer. When you're struggling with your own fears and insecurities, your prayer partner can hold your hand and intercede on your behalf. When you and your spouse are not getting along and can't get past a particular argument or sticking point, you can call a time out, drop your weapons, and go with your partner into emergency prayer. It should become your automatic reflex action when you don't know what else to do.

It's hard to stay angry long with someone for whom you're praying. It's hard not to back down when you're hearing your mate humbly cry out to God and beg Him for mercy in the midst of your heated crisis. In prayer, two people remember that God has made them one. And in the grip of His uniting presence, disharmony blends into beauty.

Praying for your spouse leads your heart to care more deeply about them. But more importantly, God is pleased when He sees you both humbling yourselves and seeking His face together. His blessing falls on you when you agree in prayer.

The word Jesus used when He talked about "agreeing" in prayer has the idea of a harmonic symphony. Two separate notes, played one at a time, sound different. They're opposed to each other. But play them at the same time — in agreement — and they can create a pleasing sense of harmony. Together they give a fuller, more complete sound than either of them can make on its own.

Agreeing in prayer is like that — even in the midst of disagreeing. It pulls you both back toward your real center. It places you on common ground, face-to-face before the Father. It restores harmony in the midst of contention.

The church — which in Scripture has a marriage connotation with Christ — can sometimes be a place where conflict rules. The disharmony that can flare up over various matters can derail the church from its mission and disrupt the free flow of worship and unity. At times godly church leaders will see what is taking place, break off discussions, and call the people of God to prayer. Instead of continuing the discord and allowing more feelings to be hurt, they will seek unity by turning their hearts back to God and appealing to Him for help.

The same thing happens in our homes when there is an intervention of prayer, even at high points of disagreement. It stops the bleeding. It quiets the loud voices. It pauses you as you realize whose presence you're in.

But prayer is for a lot more than breaking up fights. Prayer is a privilege to be enjoyed on a consistent, daily basis. When you know that prayer time awaits you before going to bed, it will change the way you spend your evening. Even if your prayers together are typically short and to the point, this will become a standing appointment that you can orbit your day around, keeping God in the middle of everything.

It's true that beginning a habit like this can initially feel awkward and uncomfortable. Anything this powerful will surprise you with its weight and responsibility when you actually try doing it. But bear in mind that God *wants* you to engage with Him — *invites* you, in fact — and He will grow you as you take it seriously and push past those times when you don't know what to say.

You'll look back at this common thread that ran through everything from average Mondays to major decisions and be so thankful for this "one thing" that changed everything. This is one area where it's imperative that you agree to agree.

## TODAY'S DARE

ASK YOUR SPOUSE IF YOU CAN BEGIN PRAYING TOGETHER. TALK ABOUT THE BEST TIME TO DO THIS, WHETHER IT'S IN THE MORNING, YOUR LUNCH HOUR, OR BEFORE BEDTIME. USE THIS TIME TO COMMIT YOUR CONCERNS, DISAGREEMENTS, AND NEEDS BEFORE THE LORD. DON'T FORGET TO THANK HIM FOR HIS PROVISION AND BLESSING. EVEN IF YOUR SPOUSE REFUSES TO DO THIS, RESOLVE TO SPEND THIS DAILY TIME IN PRAYER YOURSELF.

__ Check here when you've completed today's dare.

What can you do to help your mate be willing for the two of you to begin praying together? If you agreed to pray together, what was it like? What did you learn from it?

_____

_____

_____

_____

_____

_____

_____

_____

_____

_____

_____

_____

_____

_____

_____

*For insight into the keys of effective prayer, see Appendix I*

*In the morning my prayer comes before You. (Psalm 88:13)*

# Day 38

## Love Fulfills

### Dreams

Delight yourself in the Lord; and He will
give you the desires of your heart.
— Psalm 37:4

What is something your spouse would
really, really love? And how often do you
ask yourself that question?

Common sense tells us we can't give our
wife or husband everything they might like.
Our budgets and account balances tell us
we probably couldn't afford it anyway. And
even if we could, it might not be good for
us. Or for them.

But perhaps you've let "no" become too
quick a response. Perhaps you've let this
negative default setting become too rea-
soned and rational, too automatic. What if
instead of dismissing the thought, you did
your best to honor it. What might happen if
the one thing they said you'd never do for
them became the next thing you did?

Love sometimes needs to be extravagant. To go all out. It sometimes needs to set aside the technicalities and just bless because it wants to.

Is that thinking too much like a teenager? Is love like this no longer on the menu after so many years of marriage? After all, with the way your relationship might be at the moment, wouldn't it be less than genuine to indulge your spouse if your heart's not in it?

Well, how about *putting* your heart in it. How about adopting a new level of love that actually *wants* to fulfill every dream and desire you possibly can.

Hasn't God's love met needs in your heart that once seemed out of the question? You were living under such a load of sin and regret, you thought you'd never earn your way back into His good graces. But He looked at you with love and said you didn't have to. He wanted you back. He wanted you to realize your need for Him, and that as you repented and turned to Him, He would love and forgive you. "God, being rich in mercy, because of His great love with which He loved us, even when we were dead in our transgressions, made us alive together with Christ" (Ephesians 2:4–5).

You thought life was over when a certain

setback took all the wind out of your sails. You broke down and cried out to Him. You prayed like you'd never prayed before. And though it wasn't easy getting back up and walking on, you somehow survived. He met you with His promised peace "which surpasses all comprehension" (Philippians 4:7) and kept you on your feet.

It wasn't when you were behaving like an angel that God chose to pour out His love on you. It wasn't because you were so deserving that He offered you His grace. "God demonstrates His own love toward us, in that while we were yet sinners, Christ died for us" (Romans 5:8).

He's your model. He's the One your love is designed to imitate. Though you weren't a likely candidate for His love, He gave it anyway. He paid the price.

Not everything your spouse wants has a hefty price tag. Not everything he or she desires can be bought with money. Your wife may really want your time. She may really want your attention. She may really want to be treated like a lady, to know that her husband considers her his greatest treasure. She may really want to see in your eyes a love that chooses to be there no matter what.

Your husband may really want your respect. He may really want you to acknowledge him as the head of the house in front of the children. He may really want you to put your arms around his neck for no apparent reason, surprising him with a long kiss or a love note when there's not even a birthday or anniversary to justify it. He may really need to know that you still think he's strong and handsome, the way you used to.

Dreams and desires come in all shapes and sizes. But love takes careful notice of each one.

- Love calls you to listen to what your mate is saying and hoping for.
- Love calls you to remember the things that are unique to your relationship, the pleasures and enjoyments that bring a smile to the other's face.
- Love calls you to give when it would be a lot more convenient to wait.
- And love calls you to daydream about these opportunities so regularly that their desires become yours as well.

We dare you to think in terms of overwhelming your spouse with love. To surprise them by exceeding all their expectations with your kindness. It may or may not be a financial sacrifice, but it needs to reflect a heart that is willing to express itself with extravagance.

What is something your spouse would really, really love?

It's time you started living out the answer to that question.

## TODAY'S DARE

ASK YOURSELF WHAT YOUR MATE WOULD WANT IF IT WAS OBTAINABLE. COMMIT THIS TO PRAYER, AND START MAPPING OUT A PLAN FOR MEETING SOME (IF NOT ALL) OF THEIR DESIRES, TO WHATEVER LEVEL YOU POSSIBLY CAN.

__ Check here when you've completed today's dare.

What has made you resistant to fulfilling your mate's desires in the past? How would it change your relationship if they knew their dreams were a priority to you? What desires are you attempting to meet?

_____

_____

_____

_____

_____

_____

_____

_____

_____

_____

_____

_____

_____

_____

_____

_____

_____

_____

_____

_____

*God is able to make all grace abound to you. (2 Corinthians 9:8)*

# DAY 39
## LOVE ENDURES

Love never fails. — 1 Corinthians 13:8

Of all the things love dares to do, this is the ultimate. Though threatened, it keeps pursuing. Though challenged, it keeps moving forward. Though mistreated and rejected, it refuses to give up.

Love never fails.

Many times when a marriage is in crisis, the spouse who is trying to make things work will go to the other, declaring in no uncertain terms that no matter what has happened in the past, he or she is committed to this marriage. Their love can be counted on to last. They promise. But not wanting to hear this yet, the other spouse holds their position. They still want out. They don't see this marriage lasting long-term. Nor do they even want it to anymore.

The partner who has just laid his or her heart on the line, extending the olive branch, can't handle the rejection. So they withdraw their statement. "Fine. If that's the way you want it, that's the way it'll be."

But if love is really love, it doesn't waffle when it's not received the way you want it to be. If love can be told to quit loving, then it's not really love. Love that is from God is unending, unstoppable. If the object of its affection doesn't choose to receive it, love keeps giving anyway.

Love never fails.

Never.

That's what Jesus' love is like. His disciples were nothing if not unpredictable. After their final Passover meal together, when Jesus told them they would all forsake Him before the night was over, Peter declared, "Even though all may fall away because of You, I will never fall away. . . . Even if I have to die with You, I will not deny You" (Matthew 26:33, 35). All the other disciples echoed the very same promise.

But later that night, Jesus' inner circle of followers — Peter, James, and John — would sleep through Christ's agony in the garden. On the way to Christ's crucifixion, Peter would deny Him three times in the courtyard. But at that precise moment, the Bible says Jesus "turned and looked" at him (Luke 22:61). His men had failed Him —

again — within hours of their sworn promises. Yet He never stopped loving them, because He and His love are "the same yesterday and today and forever" (Hebrews 13:8).

When you have done everything within your power to obey God, your spouse may still forsake you and walk away — just as Jesus' followers did to Him. But if your marriage fails, if your spouse walks away, let it not be because you gave up or stopped loving them.

Love never fails.

Of the nine "fruits of the Spirit" listed in Galatians 5, the first of all is love. And because the unchanging Holy Spirit is its source — the same Holy Spirit who dwells in the hearts of all believers — then the love He creates in you is unchanging as well. It is based on the *will* of God, the *calling* of God, and the *Word* of God — all unchanging things. The Bible declares them "irrevocable" (Romans 11:29). "Heaven and earth will pass away, but My words will not pass away" (Luke 21:33).

Only a few days ago you were Love Dared to build your marriage on the Word of God. That's because when all else fails, the truth of God will still be standing. Along the way you have also been dared to be patient, to be unselfish, to sacrifice for your mate's needs.

These are not just loving ideas, existing in isolation. Each quality of love outlined in this book is based on the love of God, captured and expressed in the Word of God. The *unchanging* Word of God. No challenge or circumstance can occur that will ever put an expiration date on Him or His love. Therefore, your love — made of the same substance — bears the same, unchanging characteristics.

Love never fails.

So today your dare is to put your unfailing love into the most powerful, personal words you can. This is your chance to declare that no matter what imperfections exist — both in you and in your spouse — your love is greater still. No matter what they've done or how often they've done it, you choose to love them anyway. Though you've been far from steady in your treatment of them over the years, your days of being inconsistent in love are over. You accept this one man or woman as God's special gift to you, and you promise to love them until death.

You're saying to your spouse, "Even if you don't like what you're reading — even if you don't like *me* — I choose to love you anyway. Forever."

Because love never fails.

## TODAY'S DARE

SPEND TIME IN PERSONAL PRAYER, THEN WRITE A LETTER OF COMMITMENT AND RESOLVE TO YOUR SPOUSE. INCLUDE WHY YOU ARE COMMITTING TO THIS MARRIAGE UNTIL DEATH, AND THAT YOU HAVE PURPOSED TO LOVE THEM NO MATTER WHAT. LEAVE IT IN A PLACE THAT YOUR MATE WILL FIND IT.

__ Check here when you've completed today's dare.

What were some of the hesitations you had in writing this letter? How do you expect your spouse to respond to it? How did God help you in writing it, and what did the process teach you about yourself?

_____

_____

_____

_____

_____

_____

_He delights in unchanging love._
_(Micah 7:18)_

# Day 40
## Love is a Covenant

Where you go, I will go, and where you
lodge, I will lodge. Your people shall be
my people, and your God, my God.
— Ruth 1:16

Congratulations. You've reached the end of
the Love Dare — the book. But the experience and challenge of loving your mate is
something that never comes to an end. It
goes on for the rest of your life.

This book may end at Day 40. But who
says your dare has to stop? And as you view
your marriage relationship from this point
on, we challenge you to consider it a *covenant* instead of a *contract*. These two words
sound similar in meaning and intent but are
in reality much different. Seeing marriage
as a contract is like saying to your spouse,
"I take you for me and we'll see if this works
out." But realizing it as a covenant changes
it to say, "I give myself to you and commit

to this marriage for life."

There are many other differences between covenants and contracts. A *contract* is usually a written agreement based on distrust, outlining the conditions and consequences if broken. A *covenant* is a verbal commitment based on trust, assuring someone that your promise is unconditional and good for life. It is spoken before God out of love for another.

A *contract* is self-serving and comes with limited liability. It establishes a time frame for certain deliverables to be met and accomplished. A *covenant* is for the benefit of others and comes with unlimited responsibility. It has no expiration date. It is "till death do us part." A *contract* can be broken with mutual consent. A *covenant* is intended to be unbreakable.

The Bible contains several major covenants as part of the unfolding story of God's people. God made a covenant with Noah, promising never to destroy all flesh with a worldwide flood (Genesis 9:12–17). He made a covenant with Abraham, promising that an entire nation of descendents would come from his family line (Genesis 17:1–8). He made a covenant with Moses, declaring that the people of Israel would be God's permanent possession (Exodus 19:3–

6). He made a covenant with David, promising that a ruler would sit on his throne forever (2 Samuel 7:7–16). Ultimately, He made a "new covenant" by the blood of Christ, establishing an unending, unchanging legacy of forgiven sins and eternal life for those who believe in Him (Hebrews 9:15). Never once has God broken any of these covenants.

And then there's marriage — the strongest covenant on earth between two people, the pledge of a man and woman to establish a love that is unconditional and lasts a lifetime. In marriage, your wedding ring represents your covenant vows — not merely commitments you *hoped* to keep but premeditated promises, publicly spoken and witnessed by others.

As you've read numerous times in these pages, keeping this covenant is not something you can do in your own strength. There's good reason why God was the One who initiated covenants with His people. He alone is able to fulfill the demands of His own promises. He alone is able to forgive the receivers of His covenant when they fail to uphold their part of the agreement. But the Spirit of God is within you by virtue of your faith in His Son and the grace bestowed upon you in salvation. That means you now *can* exercise your role as covenant keeper, no matter what may arise to challenge your faithfulness to it.

Especially if your spouse is not in a place of receiving your love right now, the act of covenant keeping can grow more daunting with each passing day. But marriage is not a contract with escape clauses and exception wordings. Marriage is a covenant intended to cut off all avenues of retreat or withdrawal. There's nothing in all the world that should sever what God has joined together. Your love is based on covenant.

Hundreds of years after the prophet Malachi recorded these words, people are still wondering why God withholds His hand of blessing at times from their homes and marriages. " 'You say, 'For what reason?' Because the Lord has been a witness between you and the wife of your youth, against whom you have dealt treacherously, though she is your companion and your wife by covenant. . . . For I hate divorce, says the Lord, the God of Israel, and him who covers his garment with wrong, says the Lord of hosts. So take heed to your spirit, that you do not deal treacherously" (Malachi 2:14, 16).

Every marriage is called to be an earthly picture of God's heavenly covenant with His church. It is to reveal to the world the glory and beauty of God's unconditional love for us. Jesus said, "As the Father has loved me, so have I loved you. Now remain in my love" (John 15:9 NIV). Let His words inspire you to be a channel of God's love to your spouse.

The time is now, man or woman of God, to renew your covenant of love in all sincerity and surrender. Love is too holy a treasure to trade in for another, and too powerful a bond to be broken without dire consequences. Fasten your love afresh on this one the Lord has given you to cherish, prize, and honor.

Your life together is before you. Dare to take hold of it and never let go.

We dare you.

## TODAY'S DARE

WRITE OUT A RENEWAL OF YOUR VOWS AND PLACE THEM IN YOUR HOME. PERHAPS, IF APPROPRIATE, YOU COULD MAKE ARRANGEMENTS TO FORMALLY RENEW YOUR WEDDING VOWS BEFORE A MINISTER AND WITH FAMILY PRESENT. MAKE IT A LIVING TESTAMENT TO THE VALUE OF MARRIAGE IN GOD'S EYES AND THE HIGH HONOR OF BEING ONE WITH YOUR MATE.

__ Check here when you've completed today's dare.

What has God revealed to you during the Love Dare? How have your views of your marriage changed? How committed are you to God and to your spouse? Who can you share this with as a testimony?

_____

_____

_____

_____

_____

_____

_____

_____

_____

_____

_____

_____

_____

_____

_____

_____

_____

*He has remembered His covenant
forever. (Psalm 105:8)*

323

# Appendix

# APPENDIX I
## THE LOCKS AND KEYS OF EFFECTIVE PRAYER

*The effective, fervent prayer of a righteous man avails much. — James 5:16 NIV*

### THE LOCKS: TEN THINGS THAT BLOCK PRAYER

**1. Praying without Knowing God through Jesus**
*John 14:6* — Jesus said to him, "I am the way, and the truth, and the life; no one comes to the Father but through Me."

**2. Praying from an Unrepentant Heart**
*Psalm 66:18–19* NIV — "If I had cherished sin in my heart, the Lord would not have listened; but God has surely listened and heard my voice in prayer."

**3. Praying for Show**
*Matthew 6:5* — "When you pray, you are not to be like the hypocrites; for they love

to stand and pray in the synagogues and on the street corners so that they may be seen by men. Truly I say to you, they have their reward in full."

## 4. Praying Repetitive, Empty Words
*Matthew 6:7–8* — "And when you are praying, do not use meaningless repetition as the Gentiles do, for they suppose that they will be heard for their many words. So do not be like them; for your Father knows what you need before you ask Him."

## 5. Prayers Not Prayed
*James 4:2* — "You do not have because you do not ask."

## 6. Praying with a Lustful Heart
*James 4:3* — "You ask and do not receive, because you ask with wrong motives, so that you may spend it on your pleasures."

## 7. Praying while Mistreating Your Spouse.
*1 Peter 3:7* — "You husbands in the same way, live with your wives in an understanding way . . . and show her honor as a fellow heir of the grace of life, so that your

prayers will not be hindered."

## 8. Praying while Ignoring the Poor

*Proverbs 21:13* — "He who shuts his ear to the cry of the poor will also cry himself and not be answered."

## 9. Praying with Bitterness in Your Heart toward Someone

*Mark 11:25–26* — "Whenever you stand praying, forgive, if you have anything against anyone, so that your Father who is in heaven will also forgive you your transgressions. But if you do not forgive, neither will your Father who is in heaven forgive your transgressions."

## 10. Praying with a Faithless Heart

*James 1:6–8* — "But he must ask in faith without any doubting, for the one who doubts is like the surf of the sea, driven and tossed by the wind. For that man ought not to expect that he will receive anything from the Lord, being a double-minded man, unstable in all his ways."

### THE KEYS: TEN THINGS THAT MAKE PRAYER EFFECTIVE

## 1. Praying by Asking, Seeking, and Knocking

*Matthew 7:7–8, 11* — "Ask, and it will be given to you; seek, and you will find; knock, and it will be opened to you. For everyone who asks receives, and he who seeks finds, and to him who knocks it will be opened. . . . If you then, being evil, know how to give good gifts to your children, how much more will your Father who is in heaven give what is good to those who ask Him!"

## 2. Praying in Faith

*Mark 11:24* — "Therefore I say to you, all things for which you pray and ask, believe that you have received them, and they will be granted you."

## 3. Praying in Secret

*Matthew 6:6* — "But you, when you pray, go into your inner room, close your door and pray to your Father who is in secret, and your Father who sees what is done in secret will reward you."

## 4. Praying according to God's Will

*1 John 5:14* — "This is the confidence we have before Him, that, if we ask anything according to His will, He hears us."

## 5. Praying in Jesus' Name

*John 14:13–14* — "Whatever you ask in My name, that will I do, so that the Father may be glorified in the Son. If you ask Me anything in My name, I will do it."

## 6. Praying in Agreement with Other Believers

*Matthew 18:19–20* — "Again I say to you, that if two of you agree on earth about anything that they may ask, it shall be done for them by My Father who is in heaven. For where two or three have gathered together in My name, I am there in their midst."

## 7. Praying while Fasting

*Acts 14:23* — "When they had appointed elders for them in every church, having prayed with fasting, they commended them to the Lord in whom they had believed."

## 8. Praying from an Obedient Life

*1 John 3:21–22* — "Beloved, if our heart does not condemn us, we have confidence before God; and whatever we ask we receive from Him, because we keep His commandments and do the things that are pleasing in His sight."

## 9. Praying while Abiding in Christ and His Word
*John 15:7* — "If you abide in Me, and My words abide in you, ask whatever you wish, and it will be done for you."

## 10. Praying while Delighting in the Lord
*Psalm 37:4* — "Delight yourself in the Lord; and He will give you the desires of your heart."

## A SUMMARY OF THE LOCKS AND KEYS OF PRAYER
1. You must be in a right relationship with God.
2. You must be in a right relationship with other people.
3. Your heart must be right.

# APPENDIX II
# 20 QUESTIONS FOR YOUR SPOUSE

*Either on a date or during a private conversation, try using the questions below to learn more about the heart of your spouse. Allow the topics to raise additional questions that you may want to explore, but keep the mood and focus positive. Listen more than you talk.*

## PERSONAL

- What is your greatest hope or dream?
- What do you enjoy the most about your life right now?
- What do you enjoy the least about your life right now?
- What would your dream job be if you could do anything and get paid for it?
- What are some things you've always wanted to do but haven't had the opportunity yet?
- What three things would you like to do

before the next year passes?
- Who do you feel the most "safe" being with? Why?
- If you could have lunch with anyone in the world, who would it be and why?
- When was the last time you felt filled with joy?
- If you had to give away a million dollars, who would you give it to?

### MARITAL

- What are three things that I do that you really like?
- What are three things that I do that drive you crazy?
- What have I done in the past that made you feel loved?
- What have I done that made you feel unappreciated?
- What are three things that I can work on?
- Of the following things, what would make you feel most loved?

*Having your body massaged and caressed for an hour.*

*Sitting and talking for an hour about your favorite subject.*

*Having help around the house for an afternoon.*

*Receiving a very nice gift.*

*Hearing encouragement about how appreci-*
*ated you are.*

- What things in the past do you wish could be erased from ever happening?
- What is the next major decision that you think God would want us to make as a couple?
- What would you like your life to look like five years from now?
- What words would you like to hear from me more often?

Offer encouragement and a listening ear. Refuse to allow this to become an argument or time for you to criticize. Let this be a time for your mate to express themselves.

# APPENDIX III
# THE WORD OF GOD IN MY LIFE

*Let this proclamation help you to rightly approach the Word of God.*

The Bible is the Word of God.

It is holy, inerrant, infallible, and completely authoritative. (*Proverbs 30:5–6, John 17:17, Psalm 119:89*)

It is profitable for teaching, reproving, correcting, and training me in righteousness. (*2 Timothy 3:16*)

It matures and equips me to be ready for every good work. (*2 Timothy 3:17*)

It is a lamp to my feet and a light to my path. (*Psalm 119:105*)

It makes me wiser than my enemies. (*Psalm 119:97–100*)

It brings me stability during the storms of my life. (*Matthew 7:24–27*)

If I believe its truth, I will be set free. (*John 8:32*)

If I hide it in my heart, I will be protected in times of temptation. (*Psalm 199:11*)

If I continue in it, I will become a true disciple. (*John 8:31*)

If I meditate on it, I will become successful. (*Joshua 1:8*)

If I keep it, I will be rewarded and my love perfected. (*Psalm 19:7–11, 1 John 2:5*)

It is the living, powerful, discerning Word of God. (*Hebrews 4:12*)

It is the Sword of the Spirit. (*Ephesians 6:17*)

It is sweeter than honey and more desirable than gold. (*Psalm 19:10*)

It is indestructible and forever settled in Heaven. (*2 Corinthians 13:7–8, Psalm 119:89*)

It is absolutely true with no mixture of error. (*John 17:17, Titus 1:2*)

It is absolutely true about God. (*Romans 3:4, Romans 16:25, 27, Colossians 1*)

It is absolutely true about man. (*Jeremiah 17:9, Psalm 8:4–6*)

It is absolutely true about sin. (*Romans 3:23*)

It is absolutely true about salvation. (*Acts 4:12, Romans 10:9*)

It is absolutely true about Heaven and Hell. (*Revelation 21:8, Psalm 119:89*)

Lord, open my eyes that I may see truth
and my ears to hear truth.
Open my heart to receive it by faith.
Renew my mind to keep it in hope.
Surrender my will that I may live it
with love.

Remind me that I am responsible
when I hear it.
Help me desire to obey what You say
through it.
Transform my life that I may know it.

Burden my heart that I may share it.

Speak now, Lord.
Give me a passion to know and follow
Your will.
Nothing more. Nothing less. Nothing else.

# APPENDIX IV
# LEADING YOUR HEART

## What Is the Heart?

*Your Identity.* Your heart is the most important part of who you are. It is the center of your being, where the "real you" resides. "The heart of man reflects man" (Proverbs 27:19). As a person "thinks in his heart, so is he" (Proverbs 23:7 NKJV).

*Your Center.* Since your physical heart is in the center of your body and sends life-giving blood out to every living cell, the word "heart" has been used for centuries to describe the core starting place of all your thoughts, beliefs, values, motives, and convictions.

*Your Headquarters.* Your heart is the Pentagon of your operations. As a result, every area of your life is impacted by the direction of your heart.

# WHAT'S WRONG WITH FOLLOWING MY HEART?

*It's Foolish.* The world says "Follow your heart!" This is the philosophy of new age gurus, self-help seminars, and romantic pop songs. Because it sounds romantic and noble, it sells millions of records and books. The problem is that following your heart usually means chasing after whatever feels right at the moment whether or not it actually is right. It means throwing caution and conscience to the wind and pursuing your latest whims and desires regardless of what good logic and counsel are saying.

The Bible says, "He who trusts in his own heart is a fool, but he who walks wisely will be delivered" (Proverbs 28:26).

*It's Unreliable.* People forget that feelings and emotions are shallow, fickle, and unreliable. They can fluctuate depending upon circumstances. In an effort to follow their hearts, people have abandoned their jobs to reignite a lousy garage band, lost their life savings following a whim on a horse race, or left their lifelong mate in order to chase an attractive coworker who's been married twice already. What feels right in the height of sweet emotion often feels like a sour mistake a few years later. This selfish philosophy is also the source of countless divorces. It leads many to excuse themselves from their lifelong commitments because they no longer "feel in love."

*It's Corrupt.* The truth is, our hearts are basically selfish and sinful. The Bible says, "The heart is more deceitful than all else and is desperately sick; who can understand it?" (Jeremiah 17:9). Jesus said, "Out of the heart come evil thoughts, murders, adulteries, fornications, thefts, false witness, slanders" (Matthew 15:19). Unless our hearts are genuinely changed by God, they will continue to choose wrong things.

## SHOULD I EVER FOLLOW MY HEART?

King Solomon said, "A wise man's heart directs him toward the right, but the foolish man's heart directs him toward the left." (Ecclesiastes 10:2). Just as your heart can direct you toward hatred, lust, and violence, it can also be driven by love, truth, and kindness. As you walk with God, He will put dreams in your heart that He wants to fulfill in your life. He will also put skills and abilities in your heart that He wants to develop for His glory (Exodus 35:30–35). He will give you the desire to give (2 Corinthians 9:7) and to worship (Ephesians 5:19). As you put God first, He will step in and fulfill the good desires of your heart. The Bible says, "Delight yourself in the Lord; and He will give you the desires of your heart" (Psalm 37:4). But the only time you can feel good about following your heart is when you know your heart is intent on serving and pleasing God.

## WHY IS FOLLOWING MY HEART NOT ENOUGH?

Because our hearts are so subject to change and so utterly untrustworthy, the Scriptures communicate a much stronger message than "follow your heart." The Bible instructs you to *lead your heart.* This means to take full responsibility for its condition and direction. Realize that you do have control over where your heart is. You have been given the power by God to take your heart off one thing and to set it on something else. The following verses all communicate a message of leading your heart:

| | |
|---|---|
| Proverbs 23:17 | "Do not let your heart envy sinners." |
| Proverbs 23:19 | "Direct your heart in the way." |

| | |
|---|---|
| Proverbs 23:26 | "Give me your heart, my son, and let your eyes delight in my ways." |
| 1 Kings 8:61 | "Let your heart therefore be wholly devoted to the Lord our God." |
| John 14:27 | "Do not let your heart be troubled, nor let it be fearful." |
| James 4:8 | "Purify your hearts." |
| James 5:8 | "Strengthen your hearts." |

## HOW DO I LEAD MY HEART?

First, you need to understand that your heart follows your investment. Whatever you pour your time, money, and energy into will draw your heart. This was true before you were married. You wrote letters, bought gifts, and spent time together as a couple, and your heart followed. When you stopped investing as much in the relationship and started pouring yourself into other things, your heart followed you there. If you are not in love with your spouse today, it may be because you stopped investing in your spouse yesterday.

*Check your heart.* One of the keys to successfully leading your heart is to constantly be aware of where it is. Do you know what has your heart right now? You can tell by looking at where your time has gone in the past month, where your money has gone, and what you keep talking about.

*Guard your heart.* When something unhealthy tempts your heart, it is your responsibility to guard it against temptation. The Bible says, "Above all else, guard your heart, for it is the wellspring of life" (Proverbs 4:23 NIV). Don't let your heart put money or your work above your spouse and family. Don't let your heart lust after the beauty of another woman (Proverbs 6:25). The Bible says, "If riches increase, do not set your heart on them" (Psalms 62:10 NKJV).

*Set your heart.* The apostle Paul taught, "Set your hearts on things above, where Christ is seated at the right hand of God" (Colossians 3:1 NIV). It's time to identify where your heart needs to be and then choose to set your heart on those things. You say, "But I don't really *want* to invest in my marriage. I'd rather be doing this or that." I know.

You've set your heart on that in the past and you are stuck in a "follow your heart" mentality. But you don't have to let your feelings lead you any more. Lust is when you set your heart on something that is wrong and forbidden. You can choose to take your heart off the wrong things and set it on what is right.

*Invest your heart.* Don't wait until you feel like doing the right thing. Don't wait until you feel in love with your spouse to invest in your relationship. Start pouring into your marriage and investing where your heart is supposed to be. Spend time with your spouse. Buy gifts. Write letters. Go on dates. The more you invest, the more your heart will value your relationship. This is what the Love Dare is all about — forty days of leading your heart back to loving your spouse.